HŌJŌ

Samurai Warlords 1487–1590

Stephen Turnbull

Helion & Company

To Anne Rogers, in loving memory of Dave

Helion & Company Limited
Unit 8 Amherst Business Centre
Budbrooke Road
Warwick
CV34 5WE
England
Tel. 01926 499 619
Email: info@helion.co.uk
Website: www.helion.co.uk
Twitter: @helionbooks
Visit our blog http://blog.helion.co.uk/

Published by Helion & Company 2023
Designed and typeset by Serena Jones
Cover designed by Paul Hewitt, Battlefield Design (www.battlefield-design.co.uk)

Text © Stephen Turnbull 2023
Illustrations © as individually credited
Colour artwork © Emmanuel Valerio 2023
Flag artwork by Anderson Subtil © Helion & Company 2023
Maps drawn by George Anderson © Helion & Company 2023

Cover: Retainer Okabe Gonnodayū and his *sashimono* (back flag) with its unique wild boar motif. The yellow *uma jirushi* (battle standard) with the character *mu* (nothingness) indicated the presence on the battlefield of the daimyo Hōjō Ujinao. Illustration by Emmanuel Valerio.

ISBN 978-1-804513-53-8

British Library Cataloguing-in-Publication Data.
A catalogue record for this book is available from the British Library.

For details of other military history titles published by Helion & Company Limited, contact the above address, or visit our website: http://www.helion.co.uk

We always welcome receiving book proposals from prospective authors.

Contents

Introduction: The Hōjō Century

The sixteenth century in Japan has long been known as the *Sengoku Jidai*: 'The Age of Warring States', a term borrowed from Ancient Chinese history. There had been conflict and fighting aplenty during the preceding centuries of course, but somehow the collapse of central authority which followed the Ōnin War of 1467–77 ushered in an epoch that is regarded as particularly terrible, when rival daimyo (warlords) fought for patches of land to a bewildering background of alliances and betrayals. Throughout this time local areas of Japan produced their own strongmen, and this book is a military history of one of the greatest of these warrior dynasties: the Hōjō. They are known to history either as the Odawara Hōjō from the name of their headquarters, which was Odawara Castle in Sagami province, or alternatively as the Go-Hōjō ('Later Hōjō') to distinguish them from an earlier family that bore the same surname.

The Hōjō thrived and prospered in the area of Japan known as the Kantō. The name, which means 'east of the barrier', refers both to the natural barrier provided by the Hakone Mountains which divide Japan's main island neatly in two between Mount Fuji and the sea, and also to a succession of physical barriers put in place over the centuries by local rulers. One reason for the Hōjō's success was their ability to control access to the Kantō through the Hakone Mountains. As a result the Hōjō tended to avoid any actual fighting west of Hakone other than to assert their long-standing control over the Izu peninsula and to fight for Suruga. Otherwise the Hōjō's aggressive behaviour stayed within the Kantō, so that their territories expanded in a meaningful way only towards the north and the east. Their ultimate aim was always the complete control of the 'Kanhasshū' – the traditional 'Eight Provinces of the Kantō' – but the Hōjō never actually gained mastery of the whole area in spite of the overblown claims for their achievements made by later chroniclers. The provinces of Awa, Hitachi and most of Shimotsuke were always denied to them, while the western part of Kōzuke became a no-man's land at the edge of the Hōjō territories.

The Hōjō's borders were therefore vaguely delineated and fiercely contested, but when the clan's nemesis arrived it came not from any near neighbour but from far away in the west of Japan. Until that moment the Hōjō's splendid isolation in the eastern half of the country had allowed them to stay aloof from the tumultuous events that had attended the rise to

power of Oda Nobunaga (1534–82), the daimyo who had begun the process of reunifying Japan. Nobunaga was succeeded by the formidable Toyotomi Hideyoshi (1537–98), whose rapid ascent meant that developments in western Japan caused ripples at the edges of the Hōjō territory for the first time in their history.

By 1587 Hideyoshi had achieved mastery over the whole of western Honshu and the other two main Japanese islands of Shikoku and Kyushu. It was now time for him to move eastwards. Believing themselves to be secure within the mighty walls of Odawara Castle, the Hōjō treated Hideyoshi's threats with contempt, but they would learn very quickly of what he and his armies were capable. Marching at the head of a huge and unstoppable force, Hideyoshi 'broke the barrier' in 1590 and captured Odawara. The long-lasting physical division of Japan that had guaranteed the security of the Hōjō was gone forever, and the Hōjō century in the Kantō came to an abrupt end.

The Hakone Mountains provided security for the Hōjō to expand eastwards into the Kantō. In this print by Hiroshige Mount Fuji is seen in the distance beyond the strategic Hakone Pass. (Public domain)

The 'Old-Fashioned Hōjō'

In spite of their undoubted achievement in conquering much of the Kantō over five generations, the Hōjō have attracted a strange reputation for being hopelessly old-fashioned in their approach to warfare. For example, A. L. Sadler claimed in *A Short History of Japan* that Hideyoshi's victory revealed that the Hōjō leader was a 'conservative lord who had failed to realise how times had changed'.[1] That comment is perfectly valid for 1590 because of the contrast it makes between the part-time warriors of the Hōjō and the virtually professional soldiers that Hideyoshi was able to deploy against them in their tens of thousands. The Hōjō are also likely to have grown complacent because of the security provided by the Hakone Mountains and the undoubtedly strong defences of Odawara Castle, but the idea of them as simple old-fashioned warriors when compared to their peers is a very persistent one. The notion has usually been linked to their attitude towards the new military technology of European-style *teppō* (matchlock muskets, otherwise called harquebuses). Having failed to embrace modern weapons, so the argument goes, the out-of-date Hōjō found themselves 'staring down the barrel' when Toyotomi Hideyoshi advanced upon them in 1590.

The most cutting remark in this context was made in 1930 by the Japanese historian Takekoshi Yosaburō, who placed the blame for the Hōjō's defeat by Hideyoshi a full 40 years earlier, when the third daimyo Hōjō Ujiyasu (1515–71) put his family at a great disadvantage by failing to grasp current developments in firearms use. Noting that Ujiyasu had been among the first daimyo in Japan to acquire harquebuses, Takekoshi commented that 'Hōjō Ujiyasu was even then satisfied to set more importance upon bows and arrows than guns and to drill his soldiers by making them chase dogs.'[2]

A short passage in the chronicle *Hōjō Godai ki* about the manners and customs of Odawara does indeed confirm that *inuoumono* ('dog chasing') was practised by the Hōjō samurai, who loosed padded or blunted arrows from horseback at running dogs. It was a valuable pursuit that was used partly for training purposes and partly for sport. The context of the remark is however the reign of the fifth and final Hōjō daimyo Ujinao (1562–91), for whom a session of *inuoumono* was performed during a two-day spring festival of the martial arts. On the second day the proceedings were launched by the firing of harquebuses, which hardly shows contempt for firearms, nor does the passage imply that dog chasing by samurai was more highly valued than gunnery training for foot soldiers.[3]

Takekoshi did not develop his argument any further beyond setting it in the context of certain quaint customs of the Hōjō such as blackening their teeth in the manner of ancient courtiers 'so that you know the head is from a samurai', but Takekoshi's negative views of the Hōjō have influenced opinion for decades. In 1961 Sir George Sansom stated that 'their army included a large proportion of old-fashioned warriors',[4] and 20 years later Michael Birt

1   A. L. Sadler, *A Short History of Japan* (Sydney: Angus & Robertson, 1963), p.159.

2   Takekoshi Yosaburō, *The Economic Aspects of the History of the Civilisation of Japan*, vol. 1 (London: Allen and Unwin, 1930), p.411.

3   *Hōjō Godai ki*, in Hagiwara Tatsuo (ed.), *Hōjō shiryō shu* (*Sengoku Shiryō Sōsho*, vol. 1) (Tokyo: Jinbutsu Ōraisha, 1966), p.401.

4   George Sansom, *A History of Japan 1334–1615* (London: The Cresset Press, 1961), p.325.

noted the stubborn persistence of the belief that the Hōjō were old-fashioned, 'for their failure to utilise the matchlock's potential'.[5]

This present work will examine the Hōjō's century of achievement in the light of the evidence presented by the historical records, to describe their spectacular rise and fall and to evaluate in particular this notion of them as old-fashioned warriors, but if the Hōjō were indeed behind the times, to what standard are they being compared? The Hōjō became dominant in their part of Japan at a time when the nature of Japanese warfare was developing out of all recognition in a manner akin to the military revolution that was taking place in Europe. This popular academic concept – that a European military revolution happened sometime around the late sixteenth century – was originally associated with the idea of the inevitable triumph of superior Western technology over foreign peoples.[6] In recent years this aspect of the theory has been thoroughly challenged. For example, Andrade has shown that volley firing was established in China long before Europe and that the drilling of infantry, on which successful volley techniques was based, dated to at least 1387.[7] Swope and Kang also identified a Korean military revolution,[8] while Sun has shown very clearly how Chinese gunpowder technology was disseminated through Southeast Asia long before the arrival of any Europeans.[9] It would therefore be surprising not to find a similar Japanese military revolution taking place,[10] so the question becomes one of identifying any trends among the Hōjō that show them failing to keep pace with their contemporaries. I will argue that, far from being sluggish non-participants in the Japanese military revolution, the Hōjō's genuine skills in warfare (and a considerable amount of good luck) make them an excellent case study of the processes involved.

---

5   Michael Patrick Birt, *Warring States: A Study of the Go-Hōjō Daimyo and Domain, 1491–1590.* PhD Thesis, Princeton University, 1983, p.189.

6   Geoffrey Parker, *The Military Revolution: Military Innovation and the rise of the West 1500–1800* (Cambridge: Cambridge University Press, 1988).

7   Tonio Andrade, 'The Arquebus Volley Technique in China, *c.* 1560: Evidence from the Writings of Qi Jiguang', in *Journal of Chinese Military History* 4, 2015, pp.115–141.

8   Kenneth Swope, 'Crouching Tigers, Secret Weapons: Military Technology Employed during the Sino-Japanese–Korean War, 1592–1598', in *The Journal of Military History*, 69, 1, 2005, pp.11–41; Hyeokhweon Kang, 'Big Heads and Buddhist Demons: The Korean Musketry Revolution and the Northern Expeditions of 1654 and 1658', in *Journal of Chinese Military History* 2, 2013, pp.127–189.

9   Laichen Sun, 'Military Technology Transfers from Ming China and the Emergence of Northern Mainland Southeast Asia (*c.* 1390–1527)', in *Journal of Southeast Asian Studies*, vol. 34, no. 3, 2003, pp.495–517; Laichen Sun, 'Chinese Gunpowder Technology and Dai Viet, ca. 1390–1467', in Nhung Tuyet Tran and Anthony Reid (eds), *Viet Nam: Borderless Histories* (Madison: University of Wisconsin Press, 2006), pp.72–120.

10   Stephen Turnbull, 'Biting the Bullet: A Reassessment of the Development, Use and Impact of Early Firearms in Japan', in *Vulcan, The Journal of the History of Military Technology* 8, 2020, pp.26–53.

A suit of armour in *dō-maru* style, typical of the more ornate types of armour common at the time of the Hōjō's rise to power in the late fifteenth century. It consists of black-lacquered iron scales bound together to make armour plates which are then laced together with bands of red and dark blue silk braid. (ColBase: Integrated Collections Database of the National Institute for Cultural Heritage, Japan)

A Note on Sources

A wealth of material has survived about the Hōjō in the form of orders, muster lists, inventories and third party commentaries. From these we can ascertain such matters as army size, composition and general strategy, but for information about how their armies actually fought we are largely dependent on the literary genre known as *gunkimono* (war tales). These works have to be treated with some care because they retain many elements of the heroic medieval *gunkimono* like the famous *Heike Monogatari,* such as a concentration on the brave exploits of individual warriors, an exaggeration of their achievements and a tendency towards Buddhist moralising. There is also an inclination towards the use of stock phrases and some borrowing of scenes from earlier stories, but the outline of events which they present is historically reliable and fairly consistent.

Of the *gunkimono* that mention the Hōjō without concentrating fully on them, we note first *Kanhasshū kosenroku* (Battles of the Eight Kantō Provinces), a collection assembled by Makishima Akitake in 1726 from earlier sources, some of which have since been lost.[11] *Ōu Eikei gunki* (War Tales of the Northeast from the Ei[roku] to the Kei[chō] eras) – a compilation made in 1658 by Tobe Ikkansai – also makes some reference to the Hōjō in its descriptions of the northern wars that impacted the Hōjō's borders.[12] *Kōyō Gunkan*, the great literary epic of the Takeda clan, provides a useful alternative view of the Hōjō endeavours from the point of view of one of their deadliest enemies.[13] Finally in this category, *Taikō ki*, an elaborate biography of Toyotomi Hideyoshi composed by Oze Hoan (1564–1640) has several chapters about Hideyoshi's final campaign against the Hōjō.[14]

The most important sources are however two specific chronicles that concentrate almost exclusively on the Hōjō. *Hōjō ki* (The Hōjō Chronicle) by an unknown author of the early seventeenth century includes numerous

---

11 Nakamaru Kazunori (ed.), *Kanhasshū kosenroku* (*Sengoku Shiryō Sōsho*, vol. 15) (Tokyo: Jinbutsu Ōraisha, 1967). Henceforward *KK*.

12 Inamura Yoshitaka (ed.), *Ōu Eikei gunki* vols 1 and 2 (*Sengoku Shiryō Sōsho*, vols 3 and 4) (Tokyo: Jinbutsu Ōraisha, 1996).

13 Nakamura Kōya et al. (eds), *Kōyō Gunkan*, vol. 2 (Tokyo: Jinbutsu Ōraisha, 1965).

14 Yoshida Yutaka (ed.), *Taikō ki*, vol. 3 (Tokyo: Kyōikusha, 1979).

unique references to the Hōjō campaigns;[15] as does the better-known *Hōjō Godai ki* (The Hōjō Five Generations Chronicle), which may be regarded as a parallel account.[16] The latter work was composed around 1614 and first published in 1641. Its author was Miura Jōshin (1565–1644), a retainer of the Hōjō who is believed to have been present at Hideyoshi's siege of Odawara in 1590. On retirement Jōshin moved to Edo where he composed his famous work. An illustrated version appeared in 1659 with the addition of 90 fascinating and revealing illustrations.[17]

Both *Hōjō ki* and *Hōjō Godai ki* are epic tales told to a sound (if highly selective) historical background amid classic scenes of individual samurai prowess. Where both of them differ from the medieval *gunkimono* lies in their surprisingly frank treatment of unsavoury topics such as the massacre of civilians at Fukane Castle in 1498. Yet the works are also heroic tragedies, ending as they do with the suicide of the family patriarch as his castle falls. In this they echo the strand of remorseless fate that accompanies the destruction of the Taira clan in *Heike Monogatari*, an element that may even have been deliberately inserted into *Hōjō Godai ki* by Miura Jōshin. He composed his work, after all, in Edo, which Tokugawa Ieyasu made into his capital after displacing the Hōjō from that very spot. To use the Chinese expression, the 'mandate of heaven' had passed from the ill-fated Hōjō to the virtuous Tokugawa who were now ruling in their stead, with the Tokugawa playing the role of the victorious Minamoto (the genealogy that Ieyasu claimed for himself as shogun) and the Hōjō that of the doomed Taira.

In spite of their century of triumph the Hōjō are difficult subjects to illustrate pictorially. Their defeat in 1590 ensured that very few Hōjō artefacts would survive, and their status as losers also appears to have made artists reluctant to portray them. There is one notable exception of course: the 90 pictures in the 1659 edition of *Hōjō Godai ki*, and I would like to acknowledge the help of Joseph Bills in reading the calligraphic captions to the above work. I would also like to thank David Hansche for supplying pictures of the battlefield of Kōnodai, which Covid restrictions prevented me from visiting; and Anderson Subtil for creating the flags in the colour section. All the other photographs are mine unless otherwise indicated, and in the absence of colourful antique woodblock prints I am delighted that this book contains two specially commissioned pieces of artwork by Emmanuel Valerio, whose lively interpretations of the Hōjō at war have brought them so vividly to life.

---

15 *Hōjō ki*, in Hagiwara Tatsuo (ed.), *Hōjō shiryō shu* (*Sengoku Shiryō Sōsho*, vol. 1) (Tokyo: Jinbutsu Ōraisha, 1966), pp.10–214. Henceforward *HK*.

16 *Hōjō Godai ki*, in Hagiwara Tatsuo (ed.), *Hōjō shiryō shu* (*Sengoku Shiryō Sōsho*, vol. 1) (Tokyo: Jinbutsu Ōraisha, 1966), pp.215–439. Henceforward *HGDK*.

17 Stephen Turnbull, *The Samurai Art of War as illustrated in Hōjō Godai ki* (independently published, 2021).

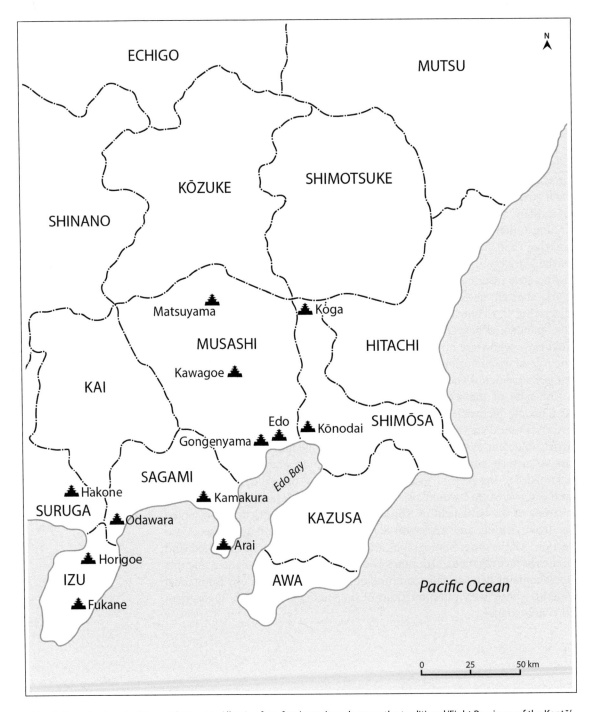

Map 1. The Kantō under Sōun and Ujitsuna. Allowing for a few boundary changes, the traditional 'Eight Provinces of the Kantō' correspond to the modern prefectures as follows. Awa, Kazusa and Shimōsa make up Chiba Prefecture; Hitachi is Ibaraki; Shimotsuke is Tochigi; Kōzuke is Gunma and Sagami is Kanagawa. Musashi is now split between Saitama Prefecture and the Metropolitan District of Tokyo, which developed out of the city of Edo.

1

The Kantō Before the Hōjō

> During all this time the Kantō, so far as any interference by Kyoto in its affairs
> was concerned, might well be considered a foreign country. It simply went its
> own way, solely occupied with its own domestic problems and with its attention
> wholly engrossed by its long and monotonous tale of intrigue, aggression, battle,
> murder and sudden death in various forms.[1]

With the above words Sir James Murdoch summed up the toxic political
environment that existed during the late fifteenth century in the area of Japan
where the Hōjō would soon come to hold sway. The factors he mentions will
be examined in detail below, but by this time the Kantō had a long history,
and 400 years earlier it had been no mere backwater of sedition. In those
days it hosted Japan's capital city because, following his victory over the Taira
clan during the Gempei War of 1180–85, Minamoto Yoritomo (1147–99)
established the first Bakufu (shogunate) at Kamakura in Sagami province.
Kamakura stayed as Japan's administrative capital until 1333, when a coup by
the Ashikaga clan led to the seat of government being moved back from the
Kantō to the ancient imperial capital of Kyoto.

The return of the capital to Kyoto after two centuries meant that there
was a need for a branch of central government to be maintained in the Kantō,
and Murdoch's comments derive from the turmoil that attended the area
when successive shoguns attempted to assert control over the eastern half
of Japan. The shogun's appointees rejoiced in the grandiose title of Kantō
Kubō ('Princes of the Kantō'). Successive Kubō had serving under them an
official known as the Kantō Kanrei ('the shogun's deputy for the Kantō'), a
position that by a quirk of history had become hereditary within the Uesugi
clan who were the dominant power in the region. The imbalance between
the two offices, an awkward relationship with the shogun and long-lasting
rivalry with the Uesugi provided the basis for over a century of turmoil.

By the beginning of the fifteenth century the Uesugi had split into three
branches: the Inukake, Ōgigayatsu and Yamanouchi, out of which Uesugi

---

1   Sir James Murdoch, *A History of Japan* vol. 1, 2nd impression (London: Kegan Paul, Trench and
    Trubner, 1925), p.627.

Zenshū (?–1417) of the Inukake had the misfortune of having to serve under the man who was probably the worst ever appointee to the post of Kantō Kubō: the headstrong Ashikaga Mochiuji (1398–1439). I have described in my book on the Ōnin War how Ashikaga Mochiuji was eliminated in 1441.[2] Only one of Mochiuji's sons escaped the massacre. He was Ashikaga Shigeuji (1434–97), and in 1449, in a desperate attempt to control eastern Japan, the reigning shogun Ashikaga Yoshimasa (1436–90) appointed Shigeuji to the post of Kantō Kubō. As had become customary, he also appointed a member of the Uesugi family to act as Shigeuji's Kantō Kanrei. It was the same formula that had failed a century earlier, and to make matters worse the appointee, Yamanouchi Uesugi Noritada (1433–54), was the son of the man who had brought about the death of Shigeuji's father.

Shigeuji thirsted for revenge and in 1454 he had Noritada killed, at which the surviving Uesugi leaders combined their branches to conduct a war against Shigeuji. More precisely, Ōgigayatsu Uesugi Mochitomo (1416–67) joined forces with Yamanouchi Uesugi Fusaaki (1432–66), the late Noritada's brother. They captured Kamakura and Ashikaga Shigeuji was forced to take refuge in the castle of Koga, where he settled for the consolation prize of the title of Koga Kubō ('Prince of Koga'). From there he and his descendants would maintain a token presence of Bakufu authority, sustained by sympathetic local daimyo who distrusted the Uesugi.

In 1459 another Ashikaga princeling joined Shigeuji in the Kantō. Shogun Yoshimasa, still desperate to retake Kamakura from the Uesugi while reining in the Koga Kubō who had failed in the effort so spectacularly, sent his half-brother Ashikaga Masatomo (1435–91) in a further attempt to impose Bakufu rule over Kamakura. Yet such was the support for the Koga Kubō and so widespread was the chaos in the Kantō that poor Masatomo never got further east than Horigoe in Izu province. Frustrated at not being able to secure Kamakura, Masatomo copied the compromise exercised by the dispossessed Shigeuji and set himself up in Horigoe Castle under the title of the Horigoe Kubō.

There were now two 'Eastern princes' in the Kantō who distrusted each other as much as they hated the Uesugi, and it is at this point that things start to get even more complicated. The Inukake branch of the Uesugi became extinct in 1461 following the death of its leader from plague. The Yamanouchi looked likely to follow them, because when the abovementioned Fusaaki died in 1466 he left only a daughter. A husband was eventually found for her from the Ōgigayatsu branch, so the Uesugi were theoretically united under this Uesugi Akisada (1454–1510), but Akisada had owed his advancement to a powerful retainer named Nagao. When that vassal died Akisada very unwisely deprived his son Nagao Kageharu of the succession. Kageharu therefore transferred his allegiance to the Ōgigayatsu branch, and civil war broke out within the Uesugi clan. By this time a new power was on the scene in the person of Hōjō Sōun (1432?–1519), the founder of an entirely new dynasty of Kantō warlords:

---

2   Stephen Turnbull, *The Ōnin War: A Turning Point in Samurai History* (Warwick: Helion, 2021), pp.36–39.

the Odawara Hōjō, for whom dissension within the Uesugi was a welcome gift. The year 1487 is usually regarded as the start of the century-long process during which Hōjō Sōun and his descendants first took on the Uesugi and then supplanted not only them but also the Kantō Kubō and other local warlords to become the undisputed masters of the Kantō.

The mounted archer was the ideal of the noble samurai warrior. As the sixteenth century went by, most mounted samurai abandoned bows in favour of edged weapons.

2

Hōjō Sōun: From Rōnin to Ruler?

The scene is described perfectly in *Hōjō ki*. There are seven samurai; they are friends and they meet one day over a cup of *sake*. Their surnames are given as Daidōji, Araki, Tame, Yamanaka, Arakawa, Aritake and Ise. A discussion develops about their future, and a pledge is made that if any one of them should achieve the status of daimyo then the other six would become his loyal retainers. The eventual winner of this strange lottery, proclaims the chronicler, was the one surnamed Ise, who is better known to history by his posthumous name of Hōjō Sōun: the first daimyo of the Odawara Hōjō.[1]

This story, which had been told about different Japanese heroes in the past, is one of several anecdotes included in the chronicles *Hōjō ki* and *Hōjō Godai ki* to add credence to the popular notion that the great Hōjō Sōun spent his early life as a *rōnin*: a wandering, masterless samurai looking for a lord to serve; hence the question mark in the title of this chapter. There are three other popular beliefs about Sōun. The first states that he was of lowly birth, while the second envisages him campaigning actively in his sixties and only dying at the advanced age of 88. The final element in the Sōun legend is the idea that all of this success was achieved because of his personal ambitions rather than at the direction of others. His life was therefore a classic application of the principle of *gekokujō* ('the low overcoming the high'), conducted over a long career from obscurity to glory. In the words of *Kamakura kanrei kudai ki* from 1672:

> He died at the age of eighty-eight. Even when he was an old man his sight and hearing were both undiminished and none of his teeth had fallen out. His hair may have grown white, but the steadiness of his mind had not changed from when he was in the prime of life. In all sincerity, everyone was deeply impressed

---

1   *HK*, pp.20–21.

by what an accomplished man he was to have lifted his family up from the lowly state of his own birth.[2]

The bare bones of the traditional 'rags to riches' version of the Sōun story are as follows. After a poor childhood and the loss of his master, Sōun acquired a position with the Imagawa clan of Suruga province. Because of his good service to the Imagawa he was rewarded with a castle, from where he took advantage of dissension in the neighbouring province of Izu to launch an ambitious invasion on his own behalf, an operation that to Murdoch exposed Sōun as no more than a 'land thief'.[3] The story continues with Sōun conquering the next province along, which was Sagami, capturing first the Hōjō's future capital of Odawara. Sōun then passed his domain on to his son Ujitsuna and died after a long and distinguished career as Japan's first *sengoku daimyō* ('lord of the warring states'): a new breed of landowning warlords who owed nothing to favours or commissions from shoguns or emperors but only to their own shrewdness and military skills.[4]

The Emergence of Ise Shinkurō

Modern research has cast considerable doubt on the traditional version of Sōun's life, and we begin with his birth. All the sources place Sōun's origins in Bitchū province, which is now part of modern Okayama Prefecture. Where the alternative accounts vary lies in the status enjoyed by his family and two widely different versions of the true year of his birth. If Sōun did indeed live to be 88 his birthdate would have been 1432, but the other date claimed for his birth is 1456, which means he would have been 64 when he died. As we will see, the earlier birth date theory is somewhat problematic because it places certain key events in his life such the birth of his heir at too advanced an age, but the belief about Sōun staying active into later life is a very popular tradition. It is also one with which the present author has a great deal of sympathy.

The specific idea that Sōun was a warrior of lowly birth who became a *rōnin* would appear to be derived largely from *Taikō ki*, the *gunkimono* based on the life of Toyotomi Hideyoshi that was first published in 1626. Hideyoshi had a similar (albeit well authenticated) rise through the ranks as that claimed for Sōun. Hence, perhaps, the fascination with Sōun's background that is entertained by its author Oze Hoan. Hoan introduces Sōun to his readers in the chapter that sets the scene for the siege of Odawara in 1590, where Hoan explains the genealogy of the family that Hideyoshi is about to fight. The current daimyo Hōjō Ujinao is, Hoan says, the fifth of the line and descended directly through a successions of firstborn sons from

---

2   *Kamakura kanrei kudai ki*, vol. 9, chapter 8 as quoted in Sugiyama Hiroshi, *Nihon no Rekishi 11: Sengoku Daimyō* (Tokyo: Chūō Kōronsha, 1974), pp.80–81.

3   Murdoch, p.628.

4   The theories about Sōun's origins and early life are summarised very thoroughly in *Hōjō Godai ki: Rekishi Gunzō Series 14* (Tokyo: Gakken, 1989), pp.38–53. Various authors.

Facing page: Hōjō Sōun (1432?–1519) was the founder of the Odawara Hōjō dynasty. He is wearing the Buddhist monk's head-dress known as a *daikoku-zukin*, which is named after Daikoku, one of the seven gods of good luck.

his great-great-grandfather Hōjō Sōun, a character initially known by his childhood name of Ise Shinkurō. Hoan claims that this man called Shinkurō was descended from Taira Kiyomori (1118–81), whose family lost out to the Minamoto in the Gempei War of the twelfth century.

Hoan stresses that Ise Shinkurō was not a high-born warrior like the Taira of old but an ordinary samurai in service to an unlucky lord in Bitchū province who was vanquished in battle, leaving 30 fighting men behind him. One of those unfortunates was Ise Shinkurō, who left Bitchū as a *rōnin* in the spring of 1457 and set out in the general direction of the Kantō on a *musha shugyō* ('warrior pilgrimage'). Hoan adds approvingly that 'he sought the spiritual help of Amaterasu Ōmikami [the goddess of the sun] and turned his steps towards Yamada in Ise. He spent 21 days there devoted to sincere prayers before he set off again.' Shinkurō's travels took him as far as Suruga province, where his military talent attracted the attention of Imagawa Yoshitada (1436–76). He was eventually accepted into the prestigious Imagawa *hatamoto* (the daimyo's personal guards: literally 'those who stand under the flag').[5]

Ise Shinkurō's service to the Imagawa is indeed well authenticated, but the alternative version of the story of how he came to join them does not portray Shinkurō as a *rōnin* escaping from a doomed daimyo. Instead his father is believed to have been an official in the Ashikaga Bakufu called Ise Morisada who had sufficient financial means to guarantee his son a good education from the monks of the Daitokuji temple in Kyoto. Morisada's position under the shogun required him to announce arrivals at the shogun's court, where he would have spent most of his time with only rare visits being made to Bitchū province. Contemporary documents mention a son called Ise Shinkurō Moritoki, who is believed to be the future Hōjō Sōun. Moritoki is the name the young man would have been given on performing his *genbuku* (coming-of-age ceremony).

At this point in the narrative the accounts of Sōun's career diverge according to the year when he is believed to have been born. If the 'great age' theory is accepted, at the age of 33 Ise Moritoki became the retainer of a very important individual: Ashikaga Yoshimi (1439–91), the younger half-brother (and sometime heir apparent) of no less a person than Ashikaga Yoshimasa, the eighth Ashikaga shogun whose name will always be linked to the terrible Ōnin War. Relations between Yoshimi and Yoshimasa deteriorated when the latter's wife gave birth to a son who would eventually become the ninth shogun Ashikaga Yoshihisa (1465–89). No longer the designated heir, Yoshimi was confined to the shogun's palace when the Ōnin War began in 1467. Not surprisingly, Yoshimi became increasingly anxious over Yoshimasa's possible decision regarding his future and left Kyoto for the safety of Ise province. He did not return to the capital until 1469. Ise Shinkurō Moritoki, it is said, accompanied Ashikaga Yoshimi in his exile. Nothing is however recorded of any service supplied to Yoshimi, and if he had been born in 1456 Moritoki would only have been nine years old when the sequence of events started, so the Yoshimi episode would have to be discounted as a myth.

---

5   Yoshida Yutaka (ed.), *Taikō ki*, vol. 3 (Tokyo: Kyōikusha, 1979), pp.10–11.

We are on firmer historical grounds when we come to the marriage of Moritoki's elder sister Kitagawa-dono ('Lady Kitagawa') to Imagawa Yoshitada (1436–76), the *shugo* (shogun's provincial deputy) of Suruga province, a happy event that probably occurred in 1467. Yoshitada had come to Kyoto to join the Eastern Army, one of the two rival factions in the Ōnin War, and it was Moritoki's father who would have announced his arrival to the shogun. These meetings led to the marriage between Yoshisada and Kitagawa-dono. A few years later (probably in 1471) Ise Moritoki took the opportunity to move to Suruga and serve his brother-in-law, either at the age of 40 or 16.

In 1473 Kitagawa-dono gave birth to a son called by his childhood name of Tatsuomaru. He was the future Imagawa Ujichika (1473–1526), but when his father Imagawa Yoshitada was killed in battle at Shiokaizaka in 1476 Tatsuomaru's rightful inheritance was placed in great peril. The rival claimant was his cousin Oshika Norimitsu, whom other retainers supported on account of Tatsuomaru's infancy. Outside interests in the shape of the Uesugi clan also plumped for Oshika Norimitsu for their own selfish reasons, but when conflict threatened the resourceful Ise Moritoki acted as a mediator in the dispute and brought all the interested parties together to work out a peaceful settlement. It is in connection with this skilful act of diplomacy that we find the name of Ise Moritoki authenticated for the first time in any historical document. Moritoki proposed that until Ujichika had performed his coming-of-age ceremony, his cousin and rival Oshika Norimitsu should act as regent and rule from the Imagawa mansion. The deal was agreed locally and vows were exchanged by drinking the sacred water of the Asama Shrine. Norimitsu accordingly moved into the Suruga capital and Tatsuomaru and his mother went to live elsewhere. The settlement would eventually be endorsed by the shogun.

Ise Moritoki's efforts had averted armed conflict in Suruga for the time being, so he returned to Kyoto and began to serve the new shogun Ashikaga Yoshihisa, who had taken over from his retired father in 1473. In 1481 we first see a document bearing the name of Ise Moritoki in the shogun's service, and by 1487 he is listed among Yoshihisa's guards, but in that same year he suddenly had to return to Suruga when Imagawa Ujichika came of age. In spite of the existence of an official document from the retired shogun Yoshimasa confirming Tatsuomaru's inheritance, Oshika Norimitsu refused to turn over control of the Imagawa clan to him and hostilities resumed. With the full support of Ujichika Ise Moritoki set up a fortified base at Ishiwaki, a place which can be regarded at the first Hōjō castle. From there on 24 November 1487 Ise Moritoki attacked Oshika Norimitsu in the fortified mansion that constituted Suruga's capital.

The operation was the future Hōjō Sōun's first fully authenticated military operation and was a complete and rapid success. It was conducted using the tactics and technology of late medieval Japan, where arrows (and not a few stones) would be the missile weapons deployed. The former would tend to be delivered by mounted horsemen, whose followers on foot were largely armed with edged weapons, of which the most popular was the *naginata*, a form of halberd. All ranks of warriors would also be armed with some form of sword. Attacks on places like the Suruga mansion almost always involved arson.

Once Oshika Norimitsu was defeated, Imagawa Ujichika took up his rightful position as the head of the clan and Moritoki received from the grateful heir the generous reward of the castle of Kōkokuji.[6] His first son Ujitsuna was born that same year, with Moritoki being then either 32 or the less likely 56. He was now a *sengoku daimyō* with an heir to his name. The dynasty that would become known as the Odawara Hōjō had come into existence.

---

6   Various authors, *Hōjō Godai ki: Rekishi Gunzō Series 14*, pp.43–45.

3

Hōjō Sōun's Dream of Greatness

Ise Shinkurō Moritoki never used the surname of Hōjō during his lifetime. It is totally retrospective and dates from the early years of his son's reign, but as this chapter covers his rise to power we will refer to him from now on as Hōjō Sōun, Sōun being the abbreviated form of the Buddhist name Ise Sōun-An Sōzui which he adopted in 1494. It is also the style used by *Hōjō Godai ki* in its retelling of the following prophetic tale.

According to this intensely symbolic story, the devout Sōun went on pilgrimage to the Mishima Grand Shrine to worship the *kami* (deity) Mishima Daimyōjin. It is unclear at which stage in his career Sōun made the visit, but while he was there he experienced a dream that would be interpreted as a prophecy of his future greatness and that of his descendants who were destined to conquer the eight provinces of the Kantō. In a vision Sōun saw an empty field where two large cedar trees were growing. The trees were eaten by a rat who then turned into a tiger. The interpretation notes that Sōun was born in the Year of the Rat and the two cedar trees (*sugi*) represented the rival Ōgigayatsu and Yamanouchi branches of the Uesugi, so it was clearly a portent of their ultimate fall at the hands of Sōun, the rat who had become a tiger. The chronicler continues by reminding his readers how the Uesugi then controlled a vast area of Japan from which they would be driven out by the Hōjō.[1]

The Invasion of Izu

Sōun's dream began to come true during the Second Year of Meiō (1493) when he invaded neighbouring Izu province in the most significant move of his entire career. It was the operation whereby the Hōjō clan began their rise to power and involved the deposition and death of the Ashikaga princeling

---

1   *HGDK*, p.238.

called the Horigoe Kubō, whose loathsome conduct made an opportunistic invasion look like the righting of a great wrong.[2]

The background is as follows. Ashikaga Masatomo, the first lord to bear the title of Horigoe Kubō, had been appointed in 1459 by his half-brother the shogun Ashikaga Yoshimasa. Masatomo died in 1491, leaving three sons by two different mothers. The older son by the first wife is known to history only by his boyhood name of Chachamaru because he never performed the traditional adult naming ceremony. The second son by a different mother called Enman-In had become a priest in the temple of Tenryūji under the name of Seikō, while her other boy was called Ashikaga Jundōji and resided with her at Horigoe.[3]

Naturally enough, as the oldest son of his late father, Chachamaru had been expecting to become the second Horigoe Kubō, but Masatomo had already ruled out Chachamaru on account of his troublesome behaviour. Chachamaru's half-brother Seikō was in a monastery, so the title passed to Jundōji and the resentful Chachamaru was imprisoned on the orders of his stepmother. There he stayed for almost two years, but Chachamaru's cause obviously found support among certain senior Ashikaga retainers because he somehow managed to break free from his incarceration. In an act of revenge that belied his youth, Chachamaru went on to murder his stepmother and half-brother Jundōji and became the new Horigoe Kubō.

The story goes on to relate that the ambitious Ise Moritoki was watching from Suruga. When he learned that many of Masatomo's old retainers were horrified by Chachamaru's actions and were seeking revenge, the future Hōjō Sōun decided to invade Izu on their behalf and oust Chachamaru. The account in *Hōjō Godai ki* of the subsequent conflict is somewhat confusing and implies that the invasion was a two-stage process. The first phase was a reconnaissance operation whereby Sōun crossed the Kisegawa and entered Izu by night. He then gathered information from a secret base at Shūzenji. The intelligence gathering was clearly worthwhile, because Sōun attacked the province at a time when many samurai from Izu were away fighting for the Uesugi. The actual invasion took place by sea from Shimizu on 10 large vessels. Sōun commanded 200 warriors of his own together with 300 provided by Imagawa Ujichika.[4] Horigoe Castle fell quickly but Chachamaru escaped, and it would take Sōun several years to track him down.

This traditional account of the affair presents the Izu invasion as a classic act of *gekokujō* carried out by an up-and-coming young samurai. His motivation appears to be no more than the natural consequence of his own desire for power but, according to historian Ienaga Junji, Hōjō Sōun's invasion was no mere local power grab. Ienaga suggests that a clue to its wider significance is provided by Sōun's decision in 1494 to have his head shaved and enter the priesthood, a seemingly personal act that had political undertones. According to Ienaga's 'conspiracy theory', the Izu invasion was

Overleaf: This illustration from a version of *Hōjō Godai ki* related to the puppet theatre shows Hōjō Sōun's dream of the rat (the Hōjō) eating two cedar trees (the Uesugi). The rat then turned into a tiger.

---

2   *HK*, pp.21–22; *HGDK*, pp.233–234.

3   Owada Tetsuo, *Imagawa Yoshimoto* (Tokyo: Minerva, 2004), p.45.

4   *HGDK*, p.234.

Hōjō Sōun leads the Izu Invasion. With the enthusiastic backing of the old Ashikaga retainers Ise Shinkurō, as he was then known, took over Horigoe Castle and added Izu Province to his own territories. It was not long afterwards that he had his head shaved and assumed the Buddhist name of Sōun.

in fact an act of revenge that Sōun was ordered to perform by Chachamaru's surviving half-brother the priest Seikō, who by then had somehow become the new shogun.[5]

Seikō owed his unexpected position to the Meiō no Seihen: the Meiō 'coup d'état'. The Meiō Coup had its origins in the unexpected death on campaign of the ninth Ashikaga shogun Yoshihisa in 1489. It had fallen to the retired shogun Yoshimasa to choose his son's successor. He selected his nephew Yoshitane, the son of his former rival Yoshimi, but in what looked like a re-run of the Ōnin War situation other leading figures backed a different nephew: Yoshitane's cousin Seikō, the priest in the Tenryūji who was the son of the Horigoe Kubō. Seikō's supporters were led by the powerful deputy shogun Hosokawa Masamoto (1466–1507), the son of the famous Katsumoto who had been the leader of the Eastern Army during the Ōnin War and was the equal of his father in political intrigue.

In accordance with Yoshimasa's wishes Ashikaga Yoshitane became the tenth Ashikaga shogun at the age of 25, but he was deposed in 1493 as a result of Hosokawa Masamoto's Meiō Coup. It began on 8 May 1493 when Hosokawa Masamoto brought Seikō out of his monastery and ordered an attack on the mansions of Yoshitane's supporters. He also assaulted the temples where Yoshitane's younger brother and sister were residing. Hosokawa Masamoto then took over Kyoto, formally deposed Yoshitane and proclaimed Seikō as shogun under the name of Ashikaga Yoshizumi.

The replacement of one shogun for another by force was an unprecedented operation that had not even been considered during the worst excesses of the Ōnin War, but Seikō/Yoshizumi was at last in a position from where he could exact revenge on Chachamaru for bringing about the death of his mother and brother. Imagawa Ujichika in the neighbouring province of Suruga was a loyal supporter of Yoshizumi's cause, and who could be more suited to carry out the act than Ujichika's talented follower Ise Moritoki? Thus it was that the future Hōjō Sōun became a government agent for an act of vengeance, performing a great service to Japan in general and to the Ashikaga family in particular by getting rid of the man who had murdered the mother of the rightful shogun.

That is the alternative theory, but whatever the overall political situation may have been, the position of Horigoe Kubō came to an abrupt end at the hands of Sōun, who gained northern Izu for himself at the invitation of the old retainers and would soon take over the entire province. At this stage in its account *Hōjō Godai ki* takes pains to assure the reader that Sōun had the welfare of the ordinary people of Izu at heart. When his army disembarked the locals thought that a pirate raid had occurred and many fled to the mountains. To reassure them Sōun arranged for the erection of notice boards in key locations forbidding the looting of abandoned properties and ordering his soldiers instead to pay for any item they seized. The regulations also stated that the rule applied to samurai dwellings as well as those of the farmers. By these statements Sōun hoped to draw former Ashikaga retainers

---

5   Ienaga Junji, *Hōjō Sōun no sujō wo sageru* (Tokyo: Shinjinbutsu Ōraisha, 2005), p.50.

to his flag, a process that was largely successful, although he gave dire warnings of what would happen if they resisted. Sōun also guaranteed laws protecting the sick, and as a result, says the chronicler with a great degree of satisfaction, Izu fell to Sōun after only 30 days. Horigoe had been destroyed during the fighting, so Sōun established himself at nearby Nirayama, which was in any case a better-defended position.

According to *Hōjō Godai ki*, Sōun's 'compassion' for the farmers of Izu who had suffered the effects of the war would be further demonstrated over the course of the next five years when he redistributed Chachamaru's lands among the local landowners rather than annexing them for himself.[6] This was of course as much pragmatism as compassion, because a wise daimyo would neither steal nor appropriate such lands; in fact a wise daimyo would not need to, because *kokujin* (provincials) like these needed the protection that a powerful daimyo could provide. They also welcomed the extra income they could receive for army service and appreciated being given increased responsibilities and honorific titles. One of the reasons for the Hōjō's future success would be their ability to transform conquered enemies like these into loyal subjects, so that farmers who once tilled the fields of their enemies happily became their own followers. The Hōjō economy would depend on them, and when the cultivators were not farming they would swell the ranks of the Hōjō army and could rise successfully through the ranks.

The Taking of Odawara

Sōun consolidated his position in Izu over the following decade while continuing to serve the Imagawa, attacking Tōtōmi province on their behalf in 1494. Sōun's personal desires were conducted to a background of threats from the dominant Uesugi and their supporters. Fortunately for Sōun, the two branches of the Uesugi spent as much time fighting each other as they did threatening him, and Sōun was sometimes able to play the two factions off against each other. In 1494, for example, Sōun offered his services to Ōgigayatsu Uesugi Sadamasa (1443–94) against his rival Yamanouchi Uesugi Akisada in a contest that ended at the disastrous battle of Arakawa. Unfortunately for Sōun, Ōgigayatsu Sadamasa fell off his horse on the battlefield and died. With his ally gone Sōun prudently withdrew his troops, but the overall alliance held, and when Sadamasa's nephew Tomoyoshi succeeded as head of the Ōgigayatsu Sōun gave him his support. Tomoyoshi established himself at Kawagoe Castle in Musashi province.

The death also occurred during that same year of 1494 of Ōmori Ujiyori, the keeper of Odawara Castle, a strategic strongpoint just over the border from Izu in Sagami. The fortress had passed into the hands of his son Fujiyori, and Sōun realised that he had been given the opportunity to expand beyond Izu and into the Kantō for the first time. According to *Hōjō ki* (for some reason *Hōjō Godai ki* makes no mention of this important episode)

---

6   *HGDK*, pp.235–236.

Sōun cultivated the young heir's friendship with gifts. One day in 1495 Sōun suggested that they go hunting for deer in the Hakone Mountains, but the beaters that Sōun brought with him were in fact his strongest troops. That night Sōun's army took up their positions to attack Odawara while confusing its garrison in an unusual manner. Sōun's forces attached burning torches to the horns of 1,000 cattle and stampeded them in the direction of Odawara Castle. The sight of numerous moving fires heading in their direction threw the Ōmori defenders into a panic, a picture which *Hōjō ki* describes very well. Sōun's samurai advanced on the main gate, swinging their long swords 'like waterwheels', and Ōmori Fujiyori was forced to respond so quickly that he went into battle wearing only half his armour. He barely escaped with his life.

Once again an operation by Sōun is popularly credited to his initiative alone, but the taking of Odawara could well have had links to the Meiō Coup because Ōmori Fujiyori favoured the dispossessed shogun Yoshitane, so Sōun may once again have been doing the government's dirty work for them. The strange 'fire-oxen' story is also likely to be a heroic elaboration of what was in essence a tale of dark treachery (the same tactic is credited to Kiso Yoshinaka in 1183), but it has entered the Hōjō story so thoroughly that representations of the terrified animals are included in the modern equestrian statue of Sōun that stands outside Odawara Station. Myths notwithstanding, Sōun captured the fortress that under his son Ujitsuna would become their future capital and provide a name for the Odawara Hōjō.[7]

---

7   *HK*, pp.32–34. Sōun chose to live at Nirayama for the rest of his days.

4

Hōjō Sōun's Last Campaigns

Odawara, the key to any advance into Sagami, had been secured, but there was still some unfinished business to sort out back in Izu. Sōun's 'stick and carrot' process – so acclaimed by Miura Jōshin – had not met with universal acclaim throughout the province, because there were elements within Izu whose primary loyalty had not been to the weak Horigoe Kubō but to the real power of the Uesugi that lay behind him, and after its accolades for Sōun's compassion *Hōjō Godai ki* plunges into the story of one of the most unsavoury episodes in the whole of the chronicle: the massacre at Fukane.

One of the greatest myths about the samurai is that warfare was carried out exclusively between honourable opponents, and that civilians were consequently spared the massacres that occurred so often in contemporary Europe. This incident disproves that notion altogether, and its inclusion in a chronicle that glorifies the Hōjō is very revealing. The Fukane episode was related to Chachamaru's surprisingly long survival. Having somehow escaped from Sōun's devastation of the Horigoe palace he had become a fugitive, seeking solace from the supporters of the ousted shogun Yoshitane. Chachamaru fondly hoped to win back control of Izu with the support of the sympathetic Uesugi and their minor retainers, who were more than willing to join his enterprise if it resulted in crushing the ambitious and expansive Hōjō Sōun. One such follower was a Uesugi retainer called Sekito Harima-no-Kami Yoshinobu, who held Fukane Castle in the south of the Izu peninsula. It was one of the few areas of Izu that were still not under Sōun's control, and the operation against it was probably linked to Sōun's determination to find and eliminate the fugitive Chachamaru. Alternative accounts tell of Chachamaru fleeing to Kai province where Sōun eventually tracked him down. The *gunkimono* place him inside Fukane in 1498 where he was killed when Sōun captured the place in a fierce attack.

Fukane was a very important gain for Hōjō Sōun because it confirmed his hold over the whole of Izu province, but the operation shows a callous side to Sōun that stands in marked contrast to the overall account of the Izu invasion. The houses of the local people were demolished and thrown into the moat to fill it up for an assault, but the ill-treatment of civilians did not stop there, because when the castle fell Sōun behaved with great brutality, beheading women, children and priests and displaying their heads on a

When Fukane castle fell Sōun behaved with great brutality, beheading women, children and priests and displaying their heads on a wooden framework outside the castle walls as a warning to others.

bamboo and wooden framework outside the castle walls as a warning to others.[1] The inclusion of this passage by Miura Jōshin strikes a very different tone from his adulatory words about Sōun's compassion, and exposes the reality of Sengoku warfare.

Another interesting notion in connection with the capture of Fukane is the suggestion that Sōun took advantage of the destruction that had been wrought by the Meiō earthquake of 1498, which is estimated to have had a magnitude of 8.0. Its epicentre was within Suruga Bay, and it caused a massive 10-metre *tsunami* that engulfed Kamakura among other places, destroying hundreds of dwellings and flooding the Great Buddha, whose sheer bulk of 112 tonnes of bronze saved it from being damaged.[2] Fukane Castle, by contrast, lost most of its defences in the tremor, so once again Sōun appears to have taken advantage of a spontaneous situation that would bring him military benefit.

Sōun and the Uesugi

In spite of the independence he had gained from the Imagawa, Sōun continued to serve the family to whom he owed so much. In 1501 he advanced as far as Mikawa province on their behalf, only to be driven back from Iwazu Castle by Matsudaira Nagachika (1473–1544), the great-great-grandfather of the future shogun Tokugawa Ieyasu.[3] Sōun's own ambitions lay very much in an easterly direction, but he struggled at first in his attempts to subdue Sagami, because with Chachamaru's death he had finally lost any pretence that the righting of that great wrong was his main aim. In addition he inevitably became entangled with the Uesugi again both as an ally and a foe. At the battle of Tachikawa ga Hara in 1504 Hōjō Sōun and Imagawa Ujichika joined forces with Ōgigayatsu Tomoyoshi and defeated an allied army of Yamanouchi Akisada and Ashikaga Masauji (1462–1531), the second Koga Kubō. Yamanouchi Akisada narrowly escaped by fleeing for his life, but he fought back and went on to capture several of the Ōgigayatsu castles.[4] Ōgigayatsu Tomoyoshi was forced back to Kawagoe, where he announced his submission to the Yamanouchi and surrendered the fortress to them. Weary from fighting, Tomoyoshi adopted his nephew Ōgigayatsu Tomooki (1488–1537) as his heir and left Kawagoe for Edo Castle, where he hoped to retire.

Tomoyoshi's change of heart made Sōun an enemy of both Uesugi branches, but fortunately for him the attentions of the Uesugi soon became drawn towards troubles they were having in their northern heartlands. In the seventh month of 1509 Yamanouchi Akisada invaded Echigo and expelled his retainer Nagao Tamekage (the father of the redoubtable samurai later known as Uesugi

---

1   *HGDK*, p.237.

2   Kitamura Akihisa et al., 'Late Holocene uplift of the Izu Islands on the northern Zenisu Ridge off Central Japan', in *Progress in Earth and Planetary Science* 4, 30, 2017, p.2.

3   Hirano Akio, *Mikawa Matsudaira ichizoku* (Tokyo: Shinjinbutsu Oraisha, 2002), p.62.

4   *HK*, pp.36–37.

Kenshin).[5] Akisada's severe style of governance in Echigo was not well received and triggered opposition by the local *kokujin*, who took the part of Tamekage and counter-attacked the following year. Akisada fought Nagao Tamekage on 25 July 1510 at the battle of Nagamorihara in Echigo.

Greatly outnumbered, Akisada killed himself at the age of 57. His adopted son Yamanouchi Uesugi Akizane (?–1515) succeeded him as Kantō Kanrei, but after returning from Echigo Akizane's adopted brother Yamanouchi Uesugi Norifusa (1466–1524) clashed with him, triggering another internal rebellion that led to further deterioration within their branch of the Uesugi clan.

Complex dissension like this was good news for Sōun and encouraged him to go raiding deep into Musashi province, but the expeditions were not successful. Tomoyoshi drove him away from Edo Castle, and another reversal happened in 1510 at Gongenyama Castle in Sagami whose keeper Ueda Masamori, a retainer of the Ōgigayatsu Uesugi, had defected to Sōun. The combined Uesugi armies rallied to besiege Gongenyama and defeated Sōun when he marched to the castle's relief on 23 August 1510. The account in *Hōjō ki's* description of Gongenyama includes one of the chronicle's first descriptions of individual combat in classic *gunkimono* style. First into the attack was the vanguard of the Uesugi under Narita Shimōsa-no-Kami, whose men tore down the brushwood defences outside the castle and raised their war cries, which elicited an appropriate response from inside the walls:

> A man from Kanagawa called Mamiya Hikoshirō, wearing a black leather suit of armour to which was fastened a *kasa-jirushi* [helmet flag] fluttering in the wind and bearing a *mon* of four open squares, opened the castle gate and cut his way out. The attacking forces sought to kill him. Loosening his left sleeve on his bow side, he struck out all round him. The soldiers inside the castle seized the opportunity and surged out, exclaiming, 'Mamiya must not be allowed to die!' For half an hour they fought, driving forwards then back again. Mamiya, who had been wounded, pulled back into the castle. The attacking force rejoiced in their victory, and the third rank joined them to press forward and rushed against the castle itself. The soldiers inside the castle closed the castle gate and confined themselves securely within it. From the ranks of the attacking force a man called Tajima Shingorō from Inate in Musashi province tried to cut the ropes that held up the gate by using his *kamayari* [cross-bladed spear]. Those inside the castle spotted him and dropped ten large stones in succession which smashed his helmet bowl and killed him. After that the troops pulled back.[6]

Sōun had to sue for a temporary peace with the Ōgigayatsu following the reversal at Gongenyama but, in spite of the setbacks he was experiencing, the evident lack of unity among the Uesugi and their supporters meant there was still a chance for Sōun to achieve mastery over the whole of Sagami, even if Musashi was totally denied to him.

---

5   *HK*, pp.37–38.

6   *HK*, pp.40–41.

Gongenyama Castle, in Musashi province, would be the site of one of Hōjō Sōun's few defeats.

江戸名所圖會

五三二

Hōjō Sōun's last campaign was against the Miura family in Arai Castle.
In this illustration the Miura heir Yoshioki charges into battle wielding a *kanasaibō*.

The Destruction of the Miura Clan

The previous years' campaigns had left only one formidable and well-established enemy within Sagami province. They were the Miura, who had ancient roots in Sagami and a distinguished record of service. In 1180 Miura Yoshiaki (1093–1181) had come to the aid of Minamoto Yoritomo after the latter's defeat by the Taira at the battle of Ishibashiyama. The family benefited greatly from Yoritomo's successful establishment of the Kamakura Bakufu and would rule their domain in Sagami for many centuries to come.

The particular Miura lord who came up against Hōjō Sōun had been adopted into the family when the current daimyo Miura Tokitaka (1416–94) failed to produce an heir. The incomer was the son of Ōgigayatsu Uesugi Takahiro, brother of the late Sadamasa who had once been Hōjō Sōun's ally. He was given the name of Yoshiatsu, but some time after his adoption a son was born. As had happened on so many other occasions in Japanese history, Miura Tokitaka disinherited Yoshiatsu and sent him to a monastery. At first Yoshiatsu accepted his fate with good grace, but in 1496 he levied troops and defeated his adoptive father in battle, taking possession of his domains and occupying Arai Castle on the Misaki Peninsula.[7] In 1499 Yoshiatsu shaved his head and took the Buddhist name of Dōsun, and the first mention of the Miura family in the context of Sōun is Dōsun's participation in the attack on Gongenyama in support of his birth family, the Ōgigayatsu Uesugi.

Both *Hōjō ki* and *Hōjō Godai ki* devote a considerable number of pages to Hōjō Sōun's operations against the Miura. This may be because the siege of Arai would be Sōun's last campaign, a siege conducted (if the 'great age' theory is accepted) when he was 86, but in any case the war has all the ingredients of a good *gunkimono* episode with dramatic suicides and related ghost stories.

When Sōun went on the offensive against Dōsun he first attacked the Miura possession of Okazaki Castle and forced them to take refuge at nearby Sumiyoshi Castle. This operation included a very symbolic bloodless victory, because in 1512 Sōun and his heir Ujitsuna were able to march unopposed into Kamakura, the former capital of Japan and the place from which the first dynasty to call themselves Hōjō had ruled. To protect their historic acquisition the new Hōjō dynasty granted tax exemptions to Kamakura's important temples, and showing a strategist's appreciation of the city's historic vulnerability built Tamanawa Castle to cover its northern approaches. Using Tamanawa as his base Sōun took Sumiyoshi, although Miura Dōsun escaped to his last outpost at Arai. This castle was built on a rocky island on the western side and was connected to the mainland by a drawbridge. A three-year standoff then began.[8]

---

7   *HK*, pp.26–28. For a full account of the Miura in the Sengoku Period see Junya Manabe, *Miura Dōsun: Ise Sōsui ni tachihadakatta saidai no raiburu* (Tokyo: Ebisu Kōshō Shuppan, 2017).

8   *HK*, pp.46–47; *HGDK*, pp.251, 254.

Miura Dōsun was supported during the siege of Arai by his giant of a son called Miura Yoshioki (1496–1516), whose name is sometimes read as Yoshimoto. Their military skills and the deployment of naval transport from their harbour below the castle kept Sōun at bay until 1516, but towards the end the castle's food supplies were running out so Sōun was able to concentrate all his resources on this last little fragment of Sagami province. The prompt for Sōun to act rapidly was the news that Ōgigayatsu Uesugi Tomooki was preparing to bring reinforcements to Arai from his castle of Edo. An all-out attack was therefore launched that broke through Arai's outer defences, and on 9 August 1516 the defeated Dōsun composed a farewell poem, drank a final cup of *sake* with his closest retainers and prepared for his end.[9]

Dōsun and Yoshioki led a final suicidal charge out of the castle gate. Yoshioki initially wielded an *ōdachi* (extra-long sword) by the famous swordsmith Masamune in a final act of defiance against Hōjō Sōun's army. His father encountered an enemy samurai called Kamiya Uta-no-Kami, whose head he cut off, but as this was to be his last battle Dōsun abandoned the trophy. After much more fighting he extricated himself from the melee and found a quiet place to commit a heroic act of *seppuku* (ritual suicide or *hara-kiri*) along with at least 15 of his closest retainers.

Hōjō ki is strangely silent on the fate of Miura Yoshioki. He is just one among a list of Dōsun's followers who are recorded as having been killed,[10] but the *Hōjō Godai ki* account of the son's end is a *tour de force*. Yoshioki was not prepared to go any more easily than his father had been, and he made his own last stand using his favourite weapon, which was a *kanasaibō* (or *bō* for short), the Japanese equivalent of a European knight's mace but constructed on a grander scale. The height of a man, a *kanasaibō* was of octagonal cross-section encased in iron strips and studded with blunt-headed nails. *Hōjō Godai ki* describes the young warrior as he emerges from the castle gate:

> Yoshioki was 21 years old and excelled all others in his ability and physique. He was seven *shaku* five *sun* tall [2.3 metres], with black whiskers and bloodshot eyes, the sinews and bones of his limbs shook violently because he possessed the strength of eighty-five men. … Wielding his *bō*, he went out of the gate alone, looking like a *yasha* (demon) emerging from a temple. He drove everyone back in all directions, knocking helmets off heads and sweeping five or even ten men to one side in one go; over five hundred were killed by being hit by his *bō*, and their corpses covered the ground leaving nowhere to step. He was like the king of the demons from the temple of death.[11]

Yoshioki was eventually overcome and resolved to follow his father in death, but no act of suicide in the whole of *Hōjō Godai ki* is as theatrical as the one he performed, because Miura Yoshioki is said to have cut off his own head. *Hōjō Godai ki* describes the act in breathless detail. Having discarded

---

9   *HK*, p.48; *HGDK*, p.256.

10   *HK*, p.48.

11   *HGDK*, p.258.

his *kanasaibō*, Yoshioki seized his pigtail in his left hand, swung his sword and decapitated himself, but that was not the end of the story, because *Hōjō Godai ki* goes on to relate how the severed head then seemed to acquire a life of its own:

> When all were utterly defeated by his wrath, with no enemies left, he cut off his own head and perished. Yet the head appeared not to be dead, the eyes seemed to be upside down and the devil's whiskers were as if they had been freshly shaved, his teeth were clenched, and the glare from his staring eyes was terrible.[12]

With Yoshioki's dramatic suicide the siege of Arai was almost over, and 'the bodies of enemy and allies alike were piled up in mounds on the fields, and their blood discoloured the green grass. Of those who had survived, many committed *seppuku*.'[13] The remnants of the Miura army took to their boats and evacuated the castle. Some of them made a determined last stand on Jōgashima, an island off the southern tip of the Misaki peninsula, but the campaign ended in Hōjō Sōun's favour following mediation from local Buddhist temples. Sōun was now the master of Sagami province.

The dramatic end of the siege of Arai and the spectacular suicide of its defending commanders must have made a deep impression on the authors of *Hōjō Godai ki* and *Hōjō ki*, because both add further material about local folk beliefs associated with the conflict. The first reference appears in *Hōjō Godai ki* after its story of Yoshioki's unusual act of suicide. The site where he died was believed to be cursed, because 'for 100 *ken* in all four directions from the spot where Yoshioki died, even now rice fields are not cultivated nor is grass cut, and any cattle or horses that enter the place die. Consequently, as even the birds and beasts know better, no one will enter.'[14]

Hōjō Godai ki also relates how the severed head seemed to stay alive for a further three years. It finally found peace when a priest from Odawara recited a sutra and the angry ghost of Yoshioki agreed to become the protective *kami* of the Igami Shrine in Odawara.[15] The straightforward deification of Yoshioki in enemy territory would be nothing to be surprised about, because there are many other examples in Japan where an enemy who dies a violent death is enshrined by the victors lest he become an angry ghost and go round causing havoc. A later elaboration of the Yoshioki story, however, adds fantastic detail to what would otherwise be an unremarkable act of protective enshrinement. It states that the severed head made its own way to Odawara by flying through the air and landed on a pine tree in a forest. The head remained intact up in the tree, frightening passers-by and seemingly immune from the prayers of visiting priests until it tumbled to the ground three years later. At that point the sympathetic priest placated it with a sutra

---

12   *HGDK*, p.258.

13   *HGDK*, pp.256–257. Burial mounds called *gishitsuka* are still visible in the fields not far from the castle.

14   *HGDK*, p.259.

15   *HGDK*, p.258.

Defeated by the Hōjō, Miura Yoshioki defiantly cuts off his own head. According to legend the severed head acquired a life of its own and terrorised the Hōjō for some time to come.

and established the Igami Shrine with Miura Yoshioki as its resident *kami*. The shrine is still venerated, although in 2018 a noticeboard which included the legend of the flying head was removed at the request of the residents of Miura, who felt that the story reflected badly on them.

In contrast to *Hōjō Godai ki*, *Hōjō ki* concentrates on other victims from the Miura clan whose ghosts would remain in the locality and continue to haunt the cliffs of Arai. It gives a full description of the associated beliefs, but is haughtily dismissive of the local villagers' superstitious fears:

> Over one hundred bodies littered the shore, and their blood filled the caves below the cliffs. It is said to this day that their angry ghosts remain in this place. On a dark night when the moon is obscured a cry can be heard that is the ghosts asking for food. It chills the nerves of the villagers and makes babies cry. Furthermore, the ghosts appear in front of the eyes of passers-by and speak to them. But such fears are mere foolishness.[16]

Hōjō Godai ki adds further information about strange phenomena that occurred locally on the anniversary of the battle:

> The battle took place on the 11th day of the 7th month. Even now every year on the 11th day of the 7th month clouds and mist gather over the Arai area, blotting out the sunlight. Lightning flashes from all directions and the wind moans like a fierce dog. Strange shapes appear in the heavens like scattered men and horses jumbled up all together in the empty sky.[17]

The author of *Hōjō Godai ki* concludes with a personal reflection on the curious twist of fate which meant that the Miura father and son committed suicide on the 11th day of the 7th month in the Year of the Tiger at the Hour of the Tiger, while over 70 years later Hōjō Ujimasa would commit suicide following the fall of Odawara on the 11th day of the 7th month in another Year of the Tiger and at the Hour of the Tiger.[18] The arithmetic is slightly out on several counts, but the parallels were valid: the suicide of a patriarch of a great clan after a bitter siege. Yet the year 1590 was many decades into the future, and at Arai the dynasty's founder Hōjō Sōun had fought his last battle. In 1518 he passed on the headship of the Hōjō to his son and heir Ujitsuna. Sōun died the following year on 8 September 1519 in Nirayama Castle and would be remembered as the first of Japan's great *sengoku daimyō*.

In 1518, in one of their final acts together, Sōun and Ujitsuna had introduced an official seal that bore the image of a tiger and expressed the optimistic slogan *rokuju ōon*, of which a loose but meaningful translation would be, 'Let all the people live in peace'. The *tora* (tiger) seal would stay in use until 1590, and represented the depersonalised governance by the Odawara daimyo as an institution. The oldest surviving example of a tiger document is dated 10

---

16   *HK*, p.48.

17   *HGDK*, p.259.

18   *HGDK*, p.259.

November 1518 and deals with mundane matters about impressing labour for cutting bamboo and the like, but it finishes with a statement that sums up the power that lay behind the words. The limits of any official's authority, it reminds the reader, are established by the presence of the tiger seal that links his local responsibility to the daimyo's overall control:

> Even trifling matters must be ordered by a Hōjō *tora* document. If there is no *tora* document, regardless if ordered by the district deputy or intendant, the order is not binding. If someone attempts such, record the name and report it to the daimyo. Thus it has been ordered.[19]

It is tempting to see a link between the choice of animal and the symbolism in the story of Sōun's dream with which this chapter commenced. Could it be that Miura Jōshin had the image on the official seal in mind when he wrote *Hōjō Godai ki*? Whatever the sequence of events might have been, by 1518 the Hōjō rat had indeed been transformed into the Hōjō tiger.

The tiger seal of the Hōjō, which both expressed and enforced the daimyo's authority.

19   Birt 1983, p.27.

5

Hōjō Ujitsuna: The Worthy Heir

Hōjō Ujitsuna was born in 1487 and began his reign as the second Hōjō daimyo when Sōun retired in 1518. He was the eldest of four sons. His immediate younger brother was Hōjō Ujitoki (?–1531), the first keeper of Tamanawa Castle in Sagami and the hero of the desperate defence of Kamakura in 1526. The others were Katsurayama Ujihiro and the scholar Hōjō Genan (1493–1589).

Ujitsuna's mother was distantly descended from the Kamakura Hōjō, a pedigree that provided legitimacy for the first major political decision of Ujitsuna's reign, which was to abandon the family name of Ise in favour of Hōjō. Even though Sōun had never used the name Hōjō during his lifetime Ujitsuna identified himself as the second generation of the 'Later' Hōjō, so it is from this time that his illustrious father is officially referred to as Hōjō Sōun. As for Ujitsuna's personal name, from his generation onwards all successive heirs and most of their brothers used the character 'Uji', which may have been an acknowledgement of the close relationship the family still had with the Imagawa clan and Sōun's erstwhile lord Ujichika.

The change of surname from Ise to Hōjō happened sometime during the summer of 1523 and was a gesture of defiance directed towards Ujitsuna's rivals in the Kantō. The original Kamakura Hōjō were famous for having supplanted the Minamoto shoguns and ruling Japan as a regency for two centuries. Now Ujitsuna was making the statement that the Odawara Hōjō were equivalent in authority to the current shogun's eastern representative and his nominal deputy the Kantō Kanrei. At the time of Ujitsuna's accession the shogun's rule in the Kantō was exercised only by the Koga Kubō, but it was not against him personally that the gesture was made because Ujitsuna and the incumbent Koga Kubō enjoyed cordial relations for most of their lives. Ashikaga Takamoto (1485–1535) had succeeded as third in the post in 1512, and during the 1520s he and the Hōjō fought side by side against

Hōjō Ujitsuna (1487–1541) continued his father's programme of conquest. He captured Edo Castle and was the victor at the First Battle of Kōnodai.

the Uesugi. Takamoto's son Ashikaga Haruuji (1508–60) – the fourth Koga Kubō – would marry Ujitsuna's daughter in 1540.[1]

Ujitsuna's defiant change of name did however find resonance with a different Ashikaga princeling because, unfortunately for the Ashikaga, Takamoto's younger brother Yoshiaki (?–1538) had rebelled against his own family. Yoshiaki courted support from the Mariyatsu branch of the Takeda clan who were located on the Bōsō peninsula, which consisted of the provinces of Awa, Kazusa and part of Shimōsa (modern Chiba prefecture). His military skills had impressed the Takeda when he ejected one of their rivals from the castle of Oyumi. Yoshiaki was rewarded with the castle, and took for himself the title of Oyumi Kubō. He settled in his new domain in 1518 and spent many years plotting how he might overthrow first his brother and then his nephew.

The Capture of Edo Castle

As Sōun's worthy heir, Ujitsuna continued his father's programme of conquest and several military successes would follow, among which Edo Castle would become a long-lasting prize. Prominent among the retainers of the Ōgigayatsu were the Ōta family of Musashi, but early in 1524 Ōta Suketaka (1498–1547) and his brothers declared their support for the Hōjō. This was the signal Ujitsuna needed to advance from Sagami into Musashi. His primary target was Edo Castle, the site of which is now the Imperial Palace in Tokyo. It was an important Uesugi possession, and its current keeper was Ōgigayatsu Tomooki, who had long given up all hope of a peaceful retirement. When the Hōjō army approached Edo Tomooki marched out as far as Shinagawa and waited for the enemy:

> After a little while, the vanguard from Odawara and the Uesugi vanguard under Soga Jinshirō clashed at Takanawahara in Shinagawa, their sweating horses galloped away to east and west, chasing and then returning, flags were unfurled and flown to north and south as they wound themselves round their victims. Seven or eight times the soldiers under their command struggled together. Ujitsuna held firm until at the last moment his second line came galloping up, at which they divided in two and surrounded the enemy from east and west and thoroughly defeated them. As Ujitsuna brandished his war fan, Uesugi was immediately overwhelmed and pulled back to go inside Edo Castle. Ujitsuna

---

1   *HK*, pp.51–52.

pursued the fugitives and pressed home the attack as they cried out in fear along with the war cries and the noise of the arrows.[2]

When night fell the castle gate was opened and Tomooki evacuated Edo. Ujitsuna raised his flags in the Akasaka district and according to custom raised three shouts of victory. Tomooki fled to Kawagoe with Ujitsuna's army in pursuit; they chased him as far as Itabashi.[3]

Because Edo was so far from Sagami Ujitsuna arranged for the repair of Kozukue Castle in Musashi to strengthen his line of communications back to Odawara. Kozukue thus became the first Hōjō *shijō* (support or satellite castle). It was the beginning of a system that would be the cornerstone of the Hōjō defence strategy, which was based around a network of satellite castles under trusted family members or senior retainers that radiated out from the *honjō* (main castle) of Odawara. Depending upon the size of the support castle and its place in the defensive hierarchy the garrison could be permanent, rotated, or kept as a skeleton force. In this, the initial phase of the castle network, Nirayama Castle in Izu covered the west; Tamanawa protected eastern Sagami, while across the Tamagawa in western Musashi stood Kozukue with Edo acting as the support castle for southern Musashi. The system would evolve over the years to become a means of governing conquered territories in addition to its primary purpose of defending the realm.

The Hōjō fish scale *mon* is displayed on the gable end of the temple of Sōunji in Yumoto, which was dedicated to Hōjō Sōun.

2   *HK*, pp.56–57.

3   *HK*, p.57.

The Battle of Kamakura

Following the establishment of Kozukue Castle in 1524 Hōjō Ujitsuna pulled back to Odawara, but Ōgigayatsu Tomooki joined forces with Yamanouchi Norifusa and began a supreme counter-attack, concentrating first on Hōjō sympathisers who were in charge of castles that did not lie within the new support network. These places would change hands from the Uesugi to the Hōjō and back again over the next few years. The main thrust of the Uesugi operations began late in 1524 with a move against the minor fortress of Moro Castle in Musashi. Ujitsuna left Edo in response, but entered into negotiations which resulted in the surrender of Moro to the Uesugi. He then hit back, and during April 1525 the Uesugi's castles at Shōbu and Kasai (in the north and east of Musashi province respectively) fell to Ujitsuna, and he was then able to surround strategic Kawagoe from all directions. Unfortunately, these successes meant that the Hōjō defence line was overextended, and on 9 September Ujitsuna was defeated by Tomooki at the battle of Shirakohara where the Hōjō lost over 800 men. By the start of 1526 the Uesugi had the upper hand and were ready to take the fight back into Sagami.

At this point a very serious situation developed for Ujitsuna from an entirely different direction. The above campaigns had all been conducted overland, but in 1526 an attack was launched across the sea against Tamanawa Castle. The amphibious operation was set in motion by the Satomi clan, whose domain of Awa province lay across the Uraga Strait from the Misaki peninsula. The Satomi had been in Awa for no more than half a century. Satomi Yoshizane (1417–88) hailed originally from Kōzuke province and had fought for the Kantō Kubō Ashikaga Mochiuji against the Uesugi. He escaped from the siege of Yūki Castle in 1441 and found refuge with the Miura clan in Sagami, under whose protection he was able to stay loyal to the cause of Mochiuji's son Ashikaga Shigeuji, the first Koga Kubō. The minor landowners of Awa province were supporters of the Uesugi, so Shigeuji sent Yoshizane across the strait to conquer the province. The operation provides the background story to one of the greatest Japanese novels: the fantastic epic *Hakkenden*, the story of the 'Eight Dog Warriors'.[4]

When the Hōjō defeated the Miura at Arai and began expanding into Musashi the Satomi became very concerned about the security of the their lands on the Bōsō peninsula.[5] The fall of Edo then brought Ujitsuna and the Satomi territories uncomfortably close together, and the Hōjō ownership of Edo also meant control of the waterways around it that emptied into the bay, so seaborne raids began in both directions across the Uraga Strait. In the two families' highly biased chronicles of the raids their own fleets are referred to as navies, while their opponents are scornfully dismissed as pirates.

---

4   This grand and very entertaining tale is brilliantly retold in English in Glynne Walley, *Eight Dogs, or Hakkenden. Part One – An Ill-Considered Jest* (New York: Cornell, 2021).

5   Junya Manabe, *Sengoku Edo wan no kaizoku: Hōjō suigun vs Satomi suigun* (Tokyo: Ebisu Kōshō Shuppan, 2018), pp.20–22.

The Satomi army march to engage the Hōjō in one of their numerous battles.

The biggest raid of all was launched in 1526 by the Satomi in alliance with the Oyumi Kubō Ashikaga Yoshiaki, and Tamanawa was its primary target. That the 1526 event was no mere pirate raid is shown by the fact that it was also coordinated with moves by Ōgigayatsu Tomooki, who was to advance overland on Tamanawa from the north as the Satomi proceeded from the east after making landfall at Miura. The operation under Satomi Yoshitoyo (1497–1534) was clearly a major attack on a strategic Hōjō possession, but neither *Hōjō ki* nor *Hōjō Godai ki* tells us anything about the Satomi's sea journey or the Hōjō's failure to prevent them from landing. It is left to the Satomi's own chronicler in *Bōsō Satomi Gunki* to boast about the details of the sea fighting and a clever ruse on the part of the attackers:

> Even though there was heavy archery fire from the enemy, the allies took it in turns to respond and made steady progress while the arrow exchanges continued. It was already the Hour of the Cock when Masaki and Anzai got together and exclaimed, 'Now is the moment!' They set up on the prows of the ships some dummies they prepared and dressed in armour, and as they advanced furiously and boldly the enemy used up their arrows against them. When the ships converged in a melee falling stones, spears, long swords and rakes were brought into action against the densely massed Hōjō troops. They soon realised that the dummies were not soldiers and raised their war cries, thrusting aimlessly with their weapons. A unit of 800 horsemen appeared from behind the cover of shields and advanced with

drawn swords, clambering on to the enemy ships. They fought their way inside the ornate palanquin on the Hōjō's flagship and captured the vessel.[6]

The invading forces landed and the allied armies converged on Tamanawa Castle, but the Hōjō defenders under Hōjō Ujitoki stopped them at the Kashiogawa and fought off the attack. After the battle the two sides exchanged the severed heads they had taken, and the Hōjō head mound stands proudly on the site of the castle to this day. Frustrated by this reversal after his successful sea battle, Satomi Yoshitoyo made an extraordinary decision: he would attack Kamakura in compensation for not capturing Tamanawa. Kamakura was an easy target, having no fortifications and probably without a garrison of any kind, so the Satomi troops swept in, burning temples and looting treasure. As a final gesture they burned down the great Tsurugaoka Hachiman Shrine. Unsurprisingly, this is the aspect of the raid that *Hōjō ki* emphasises alongside the heroism displayed by the Hōjō in driving the invaders back across the sea, and the words it puts into the mouth of the 'appalled' Hōjō Ujitsuna are:

> They are savage barbarians and are running riot. Our country is the Land of the Gods. What is more, the Satomi are from the Genji, Hachiman's clan. They have shown no understanding of propriety, and in carrying out this unparalleled atrocity they have paid no heed to the divine punishment that must of necessity be meted out in return for the attack that has occurred.[7]

As *Hōjō ki* explains with some satisfaction, the Hōjō army had the pleasure of becoming the immediate instrument of divine retribution. They advanced on ruined Kamakura, and the first casualty of the gods' vengeance was a general of the Satomi called Satomi Sakondaiyū who fell off his horse and died. Seeing this their commander Yoshitoyo ordered his army back to their boats. The Hōjō took to the sea and pursued them, but the wind rose as the Satomi crossed the strait and a tempest struck their fleet. Out of their vanguard 'not one man survived' and their commander only just escaped with his life.[8]

In spite of the fact that the raiders had been driven away by his army, the destruction of Kamakura was a severe loss of prestige for Hōjō Ujitsuna because he had allowed it to happen. There was also an unfortunate precedent because Kamakura was the place where the original Hōjō had been defeated in a cataclysmic battle in 1333, so it seemed that the new Hōjō were similarly unable to defend it. Over the ensuing years Ujitsuna and his successor would restore the Hachiman shrine at vast expense.

---

6 Bōsō Shōso Kankō Kai, 'Bōsō Satomi Gunki', in *Bōsō Shōso*, vol. 2: *Gunki* (Chiba: Bōsō Shōso Kankō Kai, 1950), p.333.

7 *HK*, p.61.

8 *HK*, p.61.

Above: The Tamanawa head mound contains the Hōjō samurai heads that were returned to the family by the Satomi after the battle of Kamakura in 1526.

Below: The Tsurugaoka Hachiman Shrine in Kamakura was completely destroyed during the Satomi raid of 1526. Its destruction placed a curse upon the Satomi family.

Needless to say, the wanton destruction of Japan's former capital heaped much greater opprobrium upon the head of Satomi Yoshitoyo. As the chronicler emphasised, the Satomi claimed descent from the ancient Minamoto, and now their leader has destroyed the sacred shrine dedicated the tutelary deity of the Minamoto family! As a self-defeating act of sacrilege it could hardly be bettered. The clan's long-term retribution came in the form of an internal feud. In 1533 Satomi Sanetaka, Yoshitoyo's uncle and the head of a cadet branch of the Satomi, attempted to overthrow Yoshitoyo with the help of the Hōjō, but the plot failed and Sanetaka was killed. Yoshitoyo then attacked Sanetaka's son Satomi Yoshitaka (1512–74). Yoshitaka escaped and with the help of the Hōjō he managed to drive Yoshitoyo out and seize power the following year. Yoshitoyo was cornered in his castle of Inamura and committed suicide: a fitting end to his crime of desecration. The defeat of Satomi Yoshitoyo marked the beginning of Satomi Yoshitaka's rise to power on the Bōsō peninsula as a force to challenge the Hōjō. Once established in post, he dissolved the alliance with Hōjō Ujitsuna and began to expand his own domain, seizing Kururi Castle and then turning his attention towards Shimōsa province, where further clashes with the Hōjō would happen, as we will shortly see.

Guns and Poetry

Two years after the Kamakura raid Ujitsuna became one of the first daimyo in the whole of Japan to discover new military technology in the form of primitive firearms. In 1528 or thereabouts he was presented with a short-barrelled Chinese-style handgun by a visiting *yamabushi* (mountain ascetic). 'Realising how marvellous and precious it was, he brought one back for Lord Ujitsuna and it was fired in his honourable presence', but the weapon was treated by the Hōjō only as a curio, not an instrument to change the face of war. Miura Jōshin in fact dismisses handguns as 'nothing to be afraid of', and reckons that arrows from the bow of the great archer Minamoto Tametomo from four centuries earlier would easily have surpassed handgun bullets in terms of penetrating power.[9] There are a few contemporary references elsewhere in Japan to what may have been bullet wounds from handguns, but as far as the Hōjō were concerned Japan's military revolution would have to wait a few more years.[10]

Meanwhile the Hōjō's contest with the Ōgigayatsu in Musashi province continued as before using established military technology. Among several actions Ujitsuna defeated them at the battle of Ozawahara on 6 June 1530. This was the first battle where his heir Hōjō Ujiyasu fought; he was then 16 years old.[11] The Uesugi responded in force in 1535 when Tomooki noticed the absence of Hōjō Ujitsuna from his home province and raided Sagami,

---

9   *HGDK*, pp.294–295; Turnbull, *The Samurai Art of War*, p.64.

10   Turnbull, 'Biting the Bullet', pp.32–33.

11   *HK*, p.63. The traditional Japanese way of reckoning age used here regards a child as one year old at birth.

burning Ōiso, Hiratsuka, Chigasaki, Kugenuma and other places and generally causing havoc. The raiders pulled back when Ujitsuna returned.[12]

The reason for Ujitsuna's absence from Sagami lay in the family's long relationship with the Imagawa of Suruga. At their head now stood Imagawa Ujiteru (1513–36) who requested help from Ujitsuna against Takeda Nobutora, the father of the famous Takeda Shingen. The Hōjō won a victory over the Takeda in Kai province in 1535, and not long afterwards Ujitsuna married his heir Ujiyasu to Ujiteru's daughter to cement their partnership. This was an important instance of the use of marriage to create alliances, because daughters of daimyo were a form of negotiable currency in Sengoku Japan. They were married off to potential supporters as a way of strengthening one's position or received as daughters-in-law from enemies in what was effectively a delicately disguised hostage system.

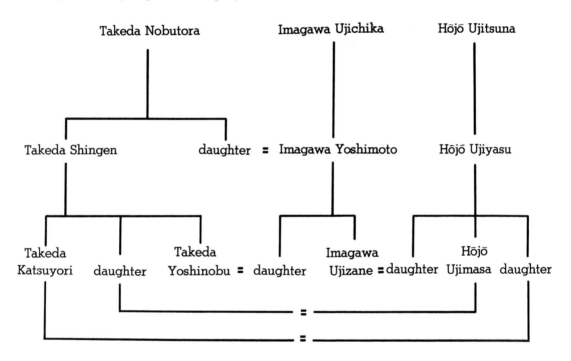

Unfortunately for the Hōjō, Imagawa Ujiteru died suddenly in 1536 and a succession dispute plunged their clan into chaos. The Hōjō backed the wrong horse in the race, and when Ujiteru's brother Imagawa Yoshimoto succeeded to the headship in 1537 he set up an alliance with the Takeda instead and married Takeda Shingen's daughter. The new partnership meant that the long-standing Imagawa/Hōjō friendship was over and marked the beginning of the so-called Katō War, which was fought over the area known as Katō ('East of the River', i.e. eastern Suruga). As part of his overriding strategy Ujitsuna set up alliances with certain minor lords in Tōtōmi on the Imagawa's western flank and thereby succeeded in dividing Yoshimoto's

A family tree showing the complex familial arrangements that existed between the Hōjō, Takeda and Imagawa families. The details are explained in the main text.

---

12 Various authors, *Hōjō Godai ki: Rekishi Gunzō Series 14*, p.73.

forces. As a result Ujitsuna was able to occupy the Katō area for some time to strengthen his western borders.

Meanwhile events back in Musashi had taken an important turn. Ōgigayatsu Tomooki died of illness in his castle of Kawagoe in 1537. The headship of the Ōgigayatsu branch fell upon 13-year-old Tomosada (1525–46), who up to then had been a novice monk. His father's last request to young Tomosada was to fight the Hōjō rather than continuing to pursue the practice of Buddhism. This Tomosada did with some enthusiasm, although he was initially forced to rely on the military experience and expertise of his uncle Ōgigayatsu Tomoshige, the late Tomooki's younger brother. To strengthen his position in Musashi province Tomosada repaired and refortified an old castle called Jindaiji. Claiming that this was an act of provocation, Ujitsuna entered Musashi and engaged Tomosada and Tomoshige at the battle of Mitsugihara, a place about five kilometres from Kawagoe, early in the morning of 20 August 1537. *Hōjō Godai ki* provides a lyrical description of the battlefield:

> The field where men and horses were arrayed was in no way physically constricted; one could not have asked for a more suitable scene for bloodshed. Flags were raised with one accord, and the forces under the two generals gathered like clouds of mist. They waited for a while for the appearance of the dragon star of good fortune [i.e. the planet Mercury], and time passed as they waited to give battle. Finally the hour drew near, and just at that moment a full moon of unprecedented brightness came out, making the dewdrops sparkle on the grass, and the insects in their dwellings in the beautiful fields of crimson brocade raised their song beneath the flowers.[13]

The tone changes as battle is joined:

> The valiant soldiers howled at the moon and rode their horses over the flowers, and very soon forgot the way of the hero. As it is written, 'they took the gongs, drums and flutes of the night and forged a tune'. Thus for some time they continued to beat the drums and raise war cries while banners flew in ecstatic clouds, but soon could be heard a sound reminiscent of the very depths of Hell. The advancing soldiers set out with the strength of Kongo Rikishi to fight like Taishaku-ten against Ashura. From all sides arrows were loosed that flew about and fell like rain; the edges of sword blades were chipped and sparks flew off them like streaks of lightning. Ten thousand flags were blown into complete disorder by the fierce wind in the empty sky, and the clamour from the men and their horses shook both heaven and earth.[14]

One hundred days had passed since Tomooki had died, and the battle of Mitsugihara was to prove a disaster for his heir Tomosada. His talented uncle Uesugi Tomoshige was taken prisoner by the Hōjō and Tomosada fled

---

13 *HGDK*, p.266.
14 *HGDK*, p.266.

the field, abandoning Kawagoe Castle to the Hōjō and seeking safety deeper inside Musashi at the fortress of Matsuyama.

Hōjō Godai ki devotes several pages of its narrative of the battle of Mitsugihara to the rival claims put forward by two samurai called Hiraiwa Hayato-no-shō and Yamaoka Buzen-no-Kami over who should have the credit for capturing Uesugi Tomoshige. It was a most unusual feat worthy of great reward, so a senior retainer who had witnessed the incident called Yamakado Shinano-no-Kami was asked to comment on the case before Ujitsuna. The legalistic Yamakado clearly believed that the matter was a complex one, and *Hōjō Godai ki* relates his long-winded argument based on historical precedent about who once did what in a similar situation many centuries ago. The passage is tedious for the modern reader, but it would have been of great interest to the audience for whom the chronicle was originally written. He talks about Minamoto Yoritomo's campaign in northeastern Japan in 1189, and brings in further instances of similarly disputed claims from the Hōgen Incident of 1156.

More usefully, Yamakado Shinano-no-Kami gave a full description of the present incident. He confirmed before Ujitsuna that he had observed Tomoshige being felled by one samurai and then taken by certain others, who then subjected their prisoner to humiliation. The precise identification of the first samurai depended on the colour of his armour and a description of his horse, both of which were supplied by other witnesses. Yamakado consequently identified Hiraiwa Hayato-no-shō, who wore an armour laced with black leather and rode a grey horse, as the samurai who had first spotted Tomoshige and suspected that he was an important general. Yamakado described how a challenge was then issued and accepted. Tomoshige was cut in the arm and forced off his horse, whereupon he was immediately seized by other Hōjō samurai who arrived eagerly on the scene. Among the latter group was Yamaoka Buzen-no-Kami, who would claim in front of Ujitsuna that it was he who should received the credit for taking Tomoshige alive. Ujitsuna concluded that Buzen-no-Kami had indeed played an important role in Tomoshige's capture, but Hiraiwa Hayato-no-shō had been the one who initially brought him down, so his part in the drama should be more highly regarded.[15]

The Hōjō now controlled the vital castle of Kawagoe. Ujitsuna placed his third son Tamemasa (1520–42) in charge of it and drew a deep breath as he advanced further into Musashi against Matsuyama, which became the site of a remarkable siege because there is supposed to have been a celebrated exchange of sarcastic poetry between the castle commander Nanbada Danjō and Yamanaka Shūzen of the besieging force. The poems involved complex puns on the rivals' allegiances and images of waves washing away the enemy. Shūzen began by riding his horse up to the castle gate (an imprint of his horse's hoof is supposed to be still visible on the volcanic rock), and proclaiming:

---

15 *HGDK*, pp.270–275; Turnbull, *The Samurai Art of War*, pp.52–55.

During the 'poetry battle' of Matsuyama Yamanaka Shūzen has fired the first volley of sarcastic verse, and awaits a rejoinder from Nanbada Danjō.

Whether or not it is wrong or right in this state of war/
Something tells me that Nanbada's beach will be swept away.

Danjō replied using words from an ancient poem about a different place called Matsuyama:

My heart goes out to your lord and master/
To even think that in the end a wave would wash over Matsuyama.[16]

Sue no Matsuyama, 'the last pine hill', is a place in Tagajō in modern Miyagi prefecture. The original poem that was adapted by Nanbada Danjō is an ode of love where the writer pledges that he is no more likely be unfaithful than for the waves of the sea to cover the hill: an impossibility because Sue no Matsuyama was the highest point of the ridge away from the ocean.[17] After this elegant exchange the Hōjō army pressed forward into the attack and burned villages round about, but the resistance from Matsuyama was too strong and Ujitsuna was forced to withdraw. Matsuyama would stay out of Hōjō hands for some years to come.

The First Battle of Kōnodai

The capture of Kawagoe and the failure at Matsuyama led to a temporary stalemate in the ongoing hostilities between the Hōjō and the Ōgigayatsu Uesugi, but within a year Hōjō Ujitsuna would be fighting against a different enemy in the form of Ashikaga Yoshiaki, the 'Prince of Oyumi'. He had long dreamed of taking control of the Ashikaga house in this part of Japan and restoring his family's ancient fortunes. For that to succeed he needed allies, and because the ruling Koga Kubō (at first his brother and from 1535 onwards his nephew Haruuji) were firmly allied to the Hōjō, it made sense for him to join forces with Satomi Yoshitaka of Awa province: Ujitsuna's erstwhile ally, now his deadly enemy.

The battle of Kōnodai in 1538 was the first major clash between the Hōjō and the Satomi since the battle of Kamakura. Kōnodai Castle lay on a plateau next to the river that acted as an important border between the provinces of Musashi and Shimōsa. The place took its name from an incident during the life of the legendary Prince Yamato-Takeru, who was campaigning in the Kantō and observed a crane wading across the river. He therefore named the rocky bluff Kōnodai, the 'plateau of the crane'. A castle had stood there since 1479 when Ōta Dōkan fortified the heights as a base for his campaign against nearby Usui Castle.

---

16 *HGDK*, p.268.

17 It has been suggested that the image is a folk memory of a *tsunami* that hit the area in the ninth century. See Fujimi City website <https://www.city.fujimi.saitama.jp/madoguchi_shisetsu/02shisetsu/shiryoukan/nanbatajo/satsuei/TV-TOKYO20111231.html> (accessed 6 March 2022).

The view of Tokyo looking from the site of Kōnodai Castle, which lies on a bluff above the river. (Photograph by David Hansche)

The sources for the first battle of Kōnodai are a number of *gunkimono*. The short *Kōnodai senki* was composed sometime before 1575, and elements of it appear in the later accounts in *Hōjō ki* and *Hōjō Godai ki*. If one makes allowances for their overemphasis on single combat and Buddhist moralising about the outcome, these texts provide a good account of the overall course of events. The *Hōjō Godai ki* account is surprisingly brief and dwells more on the ritual of head identification that took place after the battle and another dispute over an outcome, while the most remarkable feature about *Kōnodai senki* is the absence of any reference to the Satomi presence on the battlefield. Instead it becomes a tale of the noble Hōjō fulfilling their destiny by vanquishing the villainous Oyumi Kubō. The later chronicles reinstate the Satomi to their rightful place.[18]

According to all three accounts the main body of the Hōjō army left Odawara and marched to Kōnodai via Edo. Soon they were in sight of Kōnodai Castle, from where the Satomi and Ashikaga forces could look down on them across the considerable natural defence line of the river, which in those days was known as the Ichikawa. The Hōjō began to cross by a suitable ford, and it would appear that this was located some way upstream from the castle rather than beneath its hostile gaze. The crossing point is likely to have been towards the area of modern Matsuo City, which lies between Kōnodai

---

18 Much of the present author's material about the first battle of Kōnodai has been drawn from the authoritative paper by Sybil Thornton: S. A. Thornton, '*Kōnodai senki*: Traditional Narrative and Warrior Ideology in Sixteenth-Century Japan', *Oral Tradition*, 15, 2, 2000, pp.306–376.

and another plateau known as Sagamidai. Indeed, a separate account of the conflict calls it the battle of Sagamidai, and the modern battle monument lies within the area of Matsuo City still known as Sagamidai.

Generals serving the Oyumi Kubō advised him to halt the Hōjō's advance while they were still in the process of crossing the river and had landed only a few men on the other side, but Yoshiaki, 'a warrior of reckless valour', ordered his men to march forward at a controlled and steady pace. That, he believed, would awe the Hōjō into retreating by the sheer grandeur of their display. Arrows were exchanged but little else was done to staunch the hostile flow of troops, and it was not long before the two armies came to blows. Two of the Oyumi Kubō's samurai called Shiizu and Murakami, both of whom had urged Yoshiaki to act sooner, were killed. More Hōjō samurai then crossed the river, so Satomi Yoshitaka and his senior retainer Henmi Yamashiro-no-Kami abandoned the security of the Kōnodai heights and descended to engage them. Ashikaga Yoshiaki's eldest son Yoshizumi, accompanied by his uncle Ashikaga Motoyori, pushed forward to the front of the battle, and the sight of them prompted Hōjō Ujitsuna to redouble his efforts. Yoshizumi was killed, but Motoyori stood firm against 30 assailants until he too was cut down by Yamamoto Hyōgo-no-Suke.

When the news of the deaths of his son and brother reached Yoshiaki he went mad with rage. Ignoring all the pleas from his followers to retreat the Prince of Oyumi spurred on his horse, and so fierce was his assault and so strong was his example that the Hōjō began to fall back. Gasping for breath from his exertions, Yoshiaki paused for a brief rest on top of a small hillock, where a samurai of the Hōjō called Yokoi Echizen-no-Kami spotted him. Concluding that he must be a leading commander, either from his ornate armour or from the *sashimono* Yoshiaki wore on his back, Yokoi loosed an arrow which pierced clean through the armour plates around his chest, and the Prince of Oyumi fell from his horse. *Kōnodai senki* gives a stirring account of his final moments. The wounded Yoshiaki first cut an opponent's helmeted head clean in two and then succumbed to a hail of arrows. In a passage probably taken from other *gunkimono*, Ashikaga Yoshiaki died standing up like the famous warrior monk Benkei from the twelfth century, using his long *ōdachi* sword to support his shattered body. It was only when an opponent dared to approach closely and poke his sword under Yoshiaki's helmet that the Hōjō realised that the general with the fierce staring eyes was already dead.

With the enemy commander killed the advantage swung decisively to the Hōjō. Satomi Yoshitaka was driven back and fled the field, abandoning his allies to fight another day, but the loyal Henmi Yamashiro-no-Kami fought on, having persuaded four other samurai to escape with Yoshiaki's surviving son so that their house might continue. The 'aged warrior', as Henmi describes himself, then asked a comrade to act as his second while he committed *seppuku*. Finally, even Yoshiaki's horse played a part in the unfolding tragedy and galloped all the way back to Oyumi Castle, where its distressed appearance told its own story of the death of the first and only Prince of Oyumi. Yoshiaki's family heard the beast whinnying and realised immediately what must have happened.

The head inspection after the first battle of Kōnodai. The head on a tray that Ujitsuna is examining is probably that of Ashikaga Yoshiaki, the Oyumi Kubō.

With peace restored after Kōnodai, the Koga Kubō Ashikaga Haruuji took Ujitsuna's daughter as his second wife in 1541 in another example of a profitable marriage alliance. Ujitsuna also started to develop a legal and administrative system for the domain that institutionalised the systems which under Sōun had relied mainly on the daimyo's own personality. Ujitsuna was also a fervent supporter of religious foundations and ensured the continued loyalty of Sōun's old retainers by honouring his late father at the memorial temple of Sōunji in Yumoto. Another major project was the restoration of the Tsurugaoka Hachiman Shrine in Kamakura after it had been destroyed by the Satomi. He also rebuilt the huge *torii* gate on the seashore at Yuigahama that provided its grand entrance.

Just like his father Sōun, Ujitsuna wanted to secure the family's future, and not long before his death late in 1541 he produced a written testament of five articles for the edification of Ujiyasu. The first article is an exhortation to righteousness on the part of a leader; while the second urges Ujiyasu to respect everyone for the contribution they make to the domain's welfare. The third clause warns of the example set by the Uesugi who failed to follow these principles. The key fourth article lays emphasis throughout on frugality and economy, because 'to covet the latest fashions is the sign of a frivolous man', and the testament finishes with a saying that would become proverbial: 'After a victory tighten the cords of your helmet.'[19]

---

19   Motoki Kuroda, *Sengoku Hōjō Godai* (Tokyo: Ebisu Kōshō Shuppan, 2013), p.64.

6

Hōjō Ujiyasu and the 'Three Kingdoms'

With his father's advice about frugality and preparedness to inspire him, Hōjō Ujiyasu began his reign as the third Odawara daimyo, and he did not have to wait long before he saw action. The death of a leader was always a signal for rivals to try their luck, and when Ōgigayatsu Tomosada heard of the passing of the old Hōjō lord he tried unsuccessfully to recapture Edo Castle in a half-hearted assault. Ujiyasu drove them away and then, one presumes, 'tightened the cords of his helmet'.

The Hōjō would enjoy their most prolonged period of expansion under Ujiyasu, during whose reign the family went a long way towards achieving the tantalising goal of mastery of the eight provinces of the Kantō. Ujiyasu showed that he was one of new breed of daimyo whose aims (and reach) exceeded the limitations of one or two patches of territory. Sōun and Ujitsuna had already taken enormous steps in that direction, but in Ujiyasu we see someone who shared the wider political aspirations of Takeda Shingen and Uesugi Kenshin, along with whom Ujiyasu made up the so-called 'Three Kingdoms' of Eastern Japan. These three individuals will have almost equal coverage in the present chapter, and every one of the trio had begun his rise at about the same time. In 1541, the year of Ujiyasu's accession, Takeda Shingen exiled his own father and took over their domain of Kai. Not many years later Nagao Terutora, or Uesugi Kenshin as he would later be known, imprisoned his own brother and took over the leadership of their clan in Echigo province. Hōjō Ujiyasu, the heir of his father by primogeniture rather than through any unsavoury practices, was destined to repel both Shingen and Kenshin from the walls of Odawara in two separate sieges. He also studiously avoided getting involved in any direct Takeda/Uesugi conflict but made alliances with both of them as Hōjō politics dictated.

Born in 1515, Ujiyasu is generally reckoned to be the finest of the five Hōjō lords. Although perhaps not the equal of either Shingen or Kenshin in military terms, Ujiyasu campaigned with prudence and was a fine commander on the battlefield. There is however a curious legend that he had been a coward as a child. At the age of 12 Chiyomaru (as he was then known) unexpectedly fainted when watching martial arts training (a variation of the story says that he was scared by the sound of gunfire: an impossibility for the year 1527), and was so ashamed of himself that he contemplated suicide. His mentor Shimizu Yoshimasa successfully dissuaded the young man from this drastic course of action, explaining that his youthful reaction was nothing to feel guilty about.[1]

Ujiyasu took the advice to heart, and it would later be said of Ujiyasu that he never showed his back to the enemy during a total of 36 battles, as proved by the fact that all the wounds he ever received were on the front of his body. He stayed at the helm of the Hōjō clan for 30 long years, although he officially retired in 1559 at the age of 45 and passed on the headship of the Hōjō to his son Ujimasa. Ujiyasu would nevertheless be the leader on many more battlefields, supporting his son through the many challenges that they faced.

The third generation of the Hōjō was represented by Ujiyasu (1515–71), who is generally regarded as the finest of the five lords. He was the contemporary of Takeda Shingen and Uesugi Kenshin.

Ujiyasu and Firearms

One criticism levelled at Ujiyasu is of course Takekoshi's claim that he was negligent in embracing firearms, so it is worth spending a little time examining this assertion. The famous incident whereby shipwrecked Portuguese traders are believed to have brought the first European-style harquebuses to Japan occurred two years into Ujiyasu's reign in 1543. There are likely to have been other means of transmission, but the arrival of harquebuses did not herald the immediate inception of Japan's military revolution. For almost a decade they were treated as individual weapons for sharpshooting and hunting rather than armaments that could be deployed en masse by trained infantry squads. A certain Satsuma man who went on to found the Kishiwada School of gunnery records seeing a harquebus being used for hunting during the early 1550s.[2] A letter dated 21 May 1573 from Uesugi Kenshin notes how his army were resting when they heard the sound of gunshots coming from the mountains. At first his warriors were alarmed, thinking that Takeda Shingen had come to attack them, but when they found out that a hunter had fired the gun they were able to rest more easily.[3]

The individual nature of harquebuses also made them ideal for prestigious gifts. In 1553 the current shogun Ashikaga Yoshiteru offered one to Yokose

---

1   Various authors, *Hōjō Godai ki: Rekishi Gunzō Series 14*, p.88.

2   Takehisa Udagawa, 'A photographic introduction to items from the collection', in *Rekihaku*, online magazine of the National Museum of Japanese History, no. 126, 2006, 'A Witness to History', <https://www.rekihaku.ac.jp/english/outline/publication/rekihaku/126/witness.html> (accessed 14 September 2022).

3   Udagawa, 2006.

In 1558 Okayama Yagorō was shot through his breastplate by a bullet, knocked from his horse and had his head cut off. He is the first firearms casualty to be recorded in *Hōjō Godai ki*.

Narushige, whose support he craved.[4] One can therefore easily imagine Ujiyasu regarding the harquebuses as an example of another new frivolity and taking pride in the family's tradition of frugality and contempt for mere fashion as set out in his father's legacy. Takekoshi therefore may well be right as far as Ujiyasu's initial reactions were concerned, so the question becomes one of identifying when Ujiyasu experienced a change of heart about how harquebuses should be used.

Firearms were being manufactured in Japan as well as being imported by the early 1550s, and Ujiyasu was surrounded by enemies determined to shrink the borders that the Hōjō had established. Takeda Shingen and Uesugi Kenshin in particular demonstrated a mastery of firearms technology that Hōjō Ujiyasu could not possibly have ignored. Indeed, the earliest

---

4   Takehisa Udagawa, *Teppō denrai: heiki ga kataru kinsei no tanjō* (Tokyo: Kōdansha, 2013), p.31.

reference to Shingen using harquebuses dates from 1555 when he reinforced the castle of Asahiyama with supposedly 300 of the weapons. The figure is usually accepted as being historically reliable, but it is a very large number for such an early date and has to be treated with some suspicion; one-tenth of that amount would have been more consistent with similar references.[5] As for Shingen's great rival, in 1559 Uesugi Kenshin received from shogun Ashikaga Yoshiteru a written formula for making gunpowder. The overall composition of gunpowder was of course common knowledge, but factors such as the size of the shot, the required range and the prevailing weather conditions affected the ideal blending ratio of the powder from situation to situation. This particular recipe had originally been composed by the Portuguese and was transmitted via their loyal supporter Ōtomo Sōrin. The letter is dated 2 August 1559 and the detail it contains is quite amazing. The instructions cover the selection of charcoal and the creation of a gunpowder slurry to be followed by a drying process, which was a more effective method than simply mixing the grains. Conlan notes in his translation that 'Kenshin, after receiving this recipe, engaged in a series of attacks on his rivals'.[6]

Among those rivals were the Hōjō of Odawara, and *Hōjō Godai ki* confirms that Ujiyasu became an early customer of the gunsmiths, because on some unspecified date, 'A *teppō* maker called Kuniyasu came from Sakai, furthermore, Buddhist priests from Negoro, men called Suginobō, Niōhō, Kishiwada etc., came to the Kantō'.[7] Sakai and the temple of Negoroji were important centres for the manufacture and dissemination of harquebuses. If Miura Jōshin is to be believed (the date he gives as 1558 is corrected to 1560 by his modern editor), the Hōjō suffered their first recorded casualty from harquebus fire sometime in early October in that year when Uesugi Kenshin confronted Ujiyasu near Numata in Kōzuke province. A brave samurai of the Hōjō called Okayama Yagorō was shot through the breastplate of his armour by a bullet, knocked from his horse by the impact and had his head cut off.[8]

Better evidence for Ujiyasu's deployment of firearms may be found in a letter from him to an unnamed recipient dated 22 October 1560. He reminds the landowner that his territory would be among the first to suffer from an enemy invasion. Ujiyasu is therefore sending 'harquebuses, bullets and gunpowder'.[9] No numbers are given for the weapons, but this is conclusive proof that by 1560 the Hōjō were using harquebuses in the defence of their frontier strongholds. One may therefore reasonably conclude that Ujiyasu was no different from his contemporaries in his appreciation of firearms. The military revolution in the Kantō was well under way.

---

5   Udagawa 2013, p.50.

6   Thomas Conlan, 'Not So Secret Secrets: Three Uesugi documents (komonjo) of 1559', *Komonjo*, Princeton University <http://komonjo.princeton.edu/uesugi/> (accessed 26 May 2021).

7   *HGDK*, p.295; Turnbull, *The Samurai Art of War*, p.66.

8   *HGDK*, pp.292–294.

9   Udagawa 2013, p.57.

The Night Battle of Kawagoe

We must now backtrack a little, because firearms deployment lay some time in the future when Ujiyasu fought the battle for which he will always be remembered, and about which he had been blessed by a strange omen. In 1543 a huge turtle came ashore in Sagami Bay. The locals were astonished, and even though eight men were needed to carry it they found the turtle a home in the pond of the Matsubara Daimyōjin Shrine, where it attracted much attention. Ujiyasu took a particular interest in the turtle and paid it a ceremonial visit, recalling that there had been a similar good omen during the reign of his father Ujitsuna. In 1537 on that very same beach Ujitsuna had witnessed a shoal of bonito jumping into the fishermen's boats, which must have been auspicious because not long afterwards he fought the battle of Mitsugihara and captured Uesugi Tomoshige. To the author of *Hōjō Godai ki* the turtle foretold the decisive victory Ujiyasu would gain at Kawagoe in 1545, the battle with which his military reputation will forever be linked.[10]

The Uesugi fortress of Kawagoe Castle in Musashi had been acquired by Ujitsuna after his victory at Mitsugihara in 1537. In 1545 the Ōgigayatsu leader Tomosada made up his mind to win it back, and allied himself with the Koga Kubō Ashikaga Haruuji against Ujiyasu. As Haruuji had become Ujiyasu's brother-in-law five years earlier it is clear that the former Hōjō/Ashikaga partnership was no more! Taking along Yamanouchi Norimasa (1523–79, the current Kantō Kanrei) from the other Uesugi branch he marched against Kawagoe, defended by Ujiyasu's adopted Hōjō Tsunanari (1515–1587). Tsunanari was the son of a retainer of the Imagawa, and had first been entrusted with Tamanawa Castle. In a splendid illustration of the positive side of adoption, Tsunanari's son Ujishige and his grandson Ujikatsu would also serve the Hōjō with distinction to the very end as successive leaders of the Ki-sonae ('Yellow Regiment').[11]

Despite having a garrison only 8,000 strong, Tsunanari managed to hold out against supposedly 85,000 besiegers. Hōjō Ujiyasu marched to Kawagoe's relief and a brave samurai managed to slip past the Uesugi siege lines into the castle to tell his brother that they were on their way. The relieving force was another pitifully small army, but so confident of victory was Ujiyasu that he offered a deal to Ashikaga Haruuji, whom he perceived to be the weakest of the allies. The offer was rejected, but intelligence brought back from the allied lines by *shinobi* (spies: the authentic version of ninja) suggested that the besiegers were so confident of victory that their vigilance had slackened.[12]

Ujiyasu decided to make a night attack. That would be a risky tactic at any time, but it was to be coordinated with a sortie from the castle by Tsunanari. To help matters further, Ujiyasu issued orders that no one was to waste time taking heads. The practice may have been a great samurai tradition but was

---

10 *HGDK*, pp.285–287; Turnbull, *The Samurai Art of War*, p.98.

11 Hōjō Tsunanari's given name should be more properly read as Tsunashige, although Tsunanari is acceptable. He will be referred to here as Tsunanari to avoid confusion with Tsunashige the son of Hōjō Genan, whose name, which uses a different ideograph, can only be read in that way.

12 *KK*, pp.27–28, names one of the *shinobi* leaders as the famous Kazama Kotarō.

Hōjō Tsunanari waves his war fan as he leads the sortie during the Night Battle of Kawagoe.
One of his samurai has sliced an enemy completely in two.

The ritual of head taking was fundamental to the samurai tradition. It would be temporarily suspended during the Night Battle of Kawagoe in 1545.

a time-consuming process that involved identifying the victim and noting the name of the victor, a ritual that was clearly inappropriate during a night attack. It says a great deal for the loyalty of the Hōjō samurai that they willingly suspended this most basic of samurai privileges for the common good. The defenders who sallied out of the castle also wore thin white paper 'tabards' over their armour so they could be distinguished in the dark.[13] The fighting took place over a wide area, but Ujiyasu's plans worked perfectly. The coalition against them was utterly destroyed, and Hōjō control over the Kantō was dramatically confirmed. Among the Uesugi casualties was Nanbada Danjō, the hero of the poetry battle at Matsuyama, who met an ignominious end when he was engaged in single combat in the courtyard of the temple of Tōmyōji. Somehow he lost his footing and fell into the temple's well where he drowned.[14]

13   *HK*, pp.86–87.

14   *HK*, p.86.

The Night Battle of Kawagoe, as it came to be known, marked the end of the Ōgigayatsu line of the Uesugi. It also diminished the prestige of the Yamanouchi lineage in the person of Norimasa, and worse was to come for him when Ujiyasu inflicted a further defeat upon his army at Hirai Castle in 1551. Norimasa was forced to flee to Kasugayama Castle in Echigo, where he begged for protection from his vassal Nagao Kagetora. Kagetora agreed to protect his overlord on very strict terms, forcing Norimasa to adopt him as leader of the Uesugi and to pass on to him the title of Kantō Kanrei. Kagetora also changed his name to Uesugi Terutora. The following year Terutora shaved his head and took the name of Uesugi Kenshin. In this new manifestation he would become one of the greatest warlords of Japan and troubled the Hōjō for many years to come.

This damaged painting in the Kawagoe Historical Museum shows Nanbada Danjō at Kawagoe. He is being attacked by Hōjō samurai wearing white paper tabards over their armour so that they could be identified in the darkness.

Overleaf: The battle of the Fujigawa in 1554, where Toyotomi Hideyoshi is said to have fought the Hōjō. He is said to have taken the head of Itō Hyūga-no-Kami of the Hōjō force. The Hōjō mon appears on the flags to the left of the picture.

伊藤日向守を切崩を
朝比奈泰次先陣して
駿州冨士川の合戦ま

Imagawa of Suruga: the 'Fourth Kingdom'

The proximity of Suruga province to the Takeda and Hōjō territories meant that the Imagawa became involved as a 'fourth kingdom' until their power was curtailed by their famous defeat at Okehazama in 1560 at the hands of Oda Nobunaga. In 1554, however, they were still riding high, sustained by their alliance with Takeda Shingen against the Hōjō, but that partnership would soon be replaced by a Tripartite Alliance involving the Hōjō with the help of a marriage between Ujiyasu's daughter and Imagawa Yoshimoto's heir Ujizane.

According to *Hōjō ki* Ujiyasu invaded Suruga to fight the Imagawa and the Takeda before the new alliance was formed, although the story is doubtful as there is no other supporting historical documentation.[15] The account nevertheless says that on 4 April 1554 Ujiyasu and Ujimasa left Odawara and set up camp at Ukishima ga Hara. There was some fighting across the Fujigawa in a battle that *Hōjō ki* calls the battle of Kashima where 'they sent forward ashigaru (foot soldiers), and every day there was arrow warfare'.[16] A further layer of fantasy would be added later, in the form of the remarkable tradition that the Fujigawa encounter was the first campaign in which the future Toyotomi Hideyoshi took part. In his youth Hideyoshi had a brief spell as a follower of one of the Imagawa retainers prior to his well-recorded service to Oda Nobunaga, but the battle is not mentioned in *Taikō ki*.[17] The illustrated biography of Hideyoshi called *Ehon Toyotomi kunkō ki* of 1855 nevertheless includes a picture of the action by the artist Kuniyoshi. Naturally enough, says the description, Hideyoshi did himself great credit and took the head of the distinguished general Itō Hyūga-no-Kami of the Hōjō force, so it is interesting to speculate that the future destroyer of Hōjō Ujimasa may have fought against him a full 40 years earlier!

The new Tripartite Alliance between the Hōjō, Takeda and the Imagawa greatly benefited Ujiyasu because he was facing attacks on the other side of his domain, which included more raids by the Satomi. In 1556 the Hōjō fought them at the battle of Miura Bay, an engagement affected by the weather that involved much hand-to-hand fighting with grappling-hooks and pole-arms.[18] But the fighting was not confined to the sea; in 1561 Ujiyasu and Ujimasa faced a further raid by the Satomi on Kamakura. It was by no means as devastating as the attack of 1526 that had caused Ujitsuna such embarrassment, because records kept by two Kamakura temples reveal that their monks alone successfully denied entry to the raiders.[19]

---

15 Owada Tetsuo, p.152.

16 *HK*, pp.96–98.

17 Yutaka Yoshida (ed.), *Taikō ki*, vol. 1 (Tokyo: Kyōikusha, 1979), p.60.

18 *HK*, p.100; Manabe 2018, p.22.

19 Manabe 2018, p.23.

Hōjō Sōun (1432–1519), the founder of the Hōjō dynasty, sitting in command on a battlefield. He is wearing a monk's headgear over a suit of armour of old-fashioned yoroi style in the manner of a horse archer. A reel containing a spare bowstring hangs from his sword belt. (Author's collection)

Right: Okabe Gonnodayū was a retainer of the Hōjō and took a head in battle against the Satake in 1585, but when he returned to camp he discovered that his *sashimono* with its unique wild boar motif had fallen out of its holder. Gonnodayū communicated the loss to the Satake, and boldly offered to exchange the severed head trophy for the return of his flag, a suggestion which the enemy accepted. The yellow *uma jirushi* (battle standard) with the character *mu* (nothingness) indicated the presence on the battlefield of the daimyo Hōjō Ujinao.

(Original artwork © Emmanuel Valerio 2023)

Overleaf:

This plate shows Hōjō troops wearing the extra-large *sashimono* that were intended for display and intimidation rather than for use when actually fighting. Left to right:

1. Samurai foot archer bearing the vermillion banner and streamer associated with Hōjō Sōun, *c.* 1518

2. Ashigaru spearman with *sashimono* bearing the fish scale *mon c.* 1559

3. Ashigaru harquebusier *c.* 1573

4. Ashigaru archer under Hōjō Sōun *c.* 1518

(Original artwork © Emmanuel Valerio 2023.
Based on a sketch in Nakanishi 2009, p. 53.)

Plate C

Emmanuel
08/28/2011

The warrior Hosokawa Sumimoto (1489–1520) was a contemporary of Hōjō Sōun. He is shown here in armour typical of the early years of the Hōjō and is armed with a *nagamaki*.

(ColBase: Integrated Collections Database of the National Institute for Cultural Heritage, Japan)

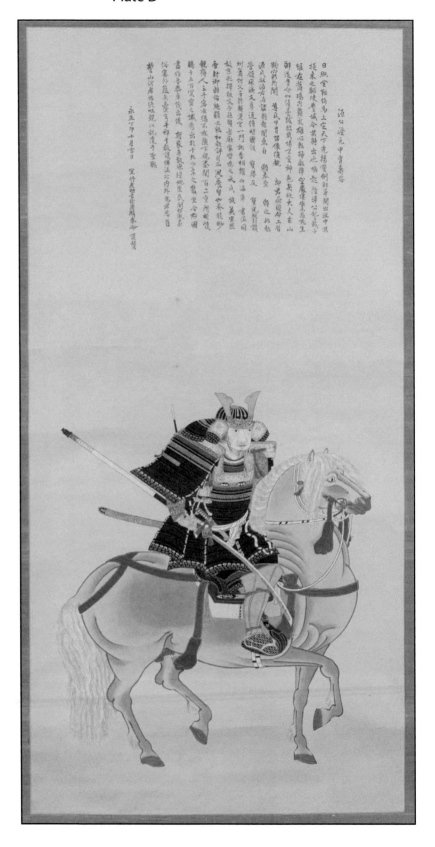

Plate E

None of the suits of armour owned by the Hōjō daimyo have survived, but this specimen is known to have been owned and worn by a contemporary of Hōjō Ujinao: Sakakibara Yasumasa (1548–1606). The use of solid plate armour is typical of the late sixteenth century and many examples would have been seen at the siege of Odawara in 1590.

(ColBase: Integrated Collections Database of the National Institute for Cultural Heritage, Japan)

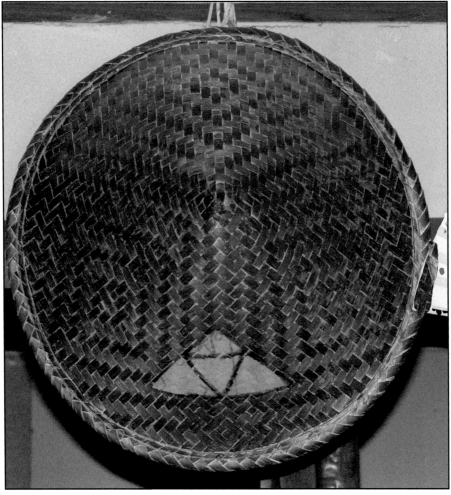

Above: Hōjō Sōun is shown here in priestly robes. His decision to take the tonsure of a Buddhist monk in 1494 was a personal act with serious political undertones. This is a modern copy in Odawara Castle of the original scroll. (Author's collection)

Facing page

Top: A typical sixteenth-century 'battledress' helmet of akoda (gourd-shaped) style with the minimum of ornamentation. Helmets like these would have been worn by many Hōjō samurai. (ColBase: Integrated Collections Database of the National Institute for Cultural Heritage, Japan)

Bottom: A jingasa ('war hat') for an ashigaru, made of lacquered basketwork and bearing the Hōjō mon, on display at a private museum on the site of Hachiōji Castle. It may well have been worn during the bloody siege of Hachiōji in 1590. (Author's photo)

This statue of Hōjō Sōun stands outside Odawara Station and depicts the legendary ruse whereby Sōun fixed burning brands to the horns of a herd of oxen and stampeded them in the direction of the castle. The defenders thought a huge army was attacking them by night, and were easily overcome. (Author's photo)

Plate I

Above: A nineteenth-century print showing the third daimyo Hōjō Ujiyasu (1515–71) in action at the second battle of Kōnodai in 1564. Note the Hōjō army crossing the river and the distant view of Mount Fuji. (Author's collection)

Below: *Inuoumono* ('dog chasing') was practised by the Hōjō samurai, who loosed padded or blunted arrows from horseback at running dogs. It was a valuable pursuit used partly for training purposes and partly for sport, but it led to the Hōjō being labelled old-fashioned warriors. (Public domain)

北条美濃守氏規

Hōjō Ujinori (1545–1600) was a brother of Ujimasa. He was instrumental in negotiations with Hideyoshi in the years leading up to the siege of 1590, and when Odawara fell he acted as Ujimasa's second when his brother committed honourable *seppuku*. In this detail from a print by Kuniyoshi he wears the *sashimono* of the Hōjō's Red Regiment. (Author's collection)

北条左太夫陸奥守平氏政朝巨

Hōjō Ujimasa (1538–90) was the fourth Hōjō daimyo. He fought many campaigns on the borders of the Hōjō territories and in 1590 faced up to the might of Toyotomi Hideyoshi. This is a detail from a print by Kuniyoshi. (Author's collection)

Plate L

Ōta Sanraku Sukemasa (1522–91) was a daimyo whose support shifted from the Hōjō to their rivals and back again on several occasions. In 1561 he defended Matsuyama Castle against a Takeda/Hōjō alliance and is famous for having used dogs as messengers. (Public domain)

Plate M

Takeda Shingen (1521–73), sometimes the Hōjō's ally and sometimes their deadliest enemy, as depicted on a painted screen in the museum of the Rinsenji where his rival Uesugi Kenshin once studied. (Author's collection)

Watanabe Kanbei (1562–1640), whose personal testimony provides a blow by blow account of the capture of the strategic castle of Yamanaka which protected the Hakone Pass. (Public domain)

Flags of the Hōjō

(Illustrations by Anderson Subtil
© Helion & Company 2023)

The five-coloured *nobori* (banner) of Hōjō Ujiyasu, representing on one flag the five 'Colour Regiments' of Ujiyasu's *karō* (senior retainers).

The *nobori* of Hōjō Ujimasa proclaiming a proverb derived from the tea ceremony whereby 'there is no cold spot to be found in boiling water' ('boiling water' is an analogy for the battlefield).

Sashimono of Ujiyasu's Red Regiment under Hōjō Tsunataka (1506–85) who was adopted by Hōjō Ujitsuna.

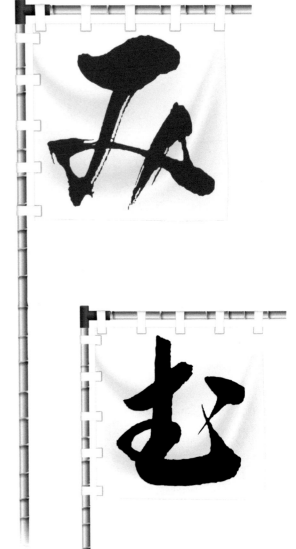

Flags of the Hōjō

Above left: The cherished *uma jirushi* bearing the name of the *kami* Hachiman that was flown by the Yellow Regiment under Hōjō Tsunanari.

Above right: A *sashimono* from one of Ujiyasu's 48 *banshō* (guard captains) each of whom was distinguished by a different character from the Japanese syllabary written in the *hiragana* style. This one bears the character *mi* (the characters *mi*, *shi*, [*w*]*e*, *hi*, *mo*, *se* and *su* were depicted in red).

Right: Another of the 48 *banshō*, this one bearing the character *mu* in black.

(Illustrations by Anderson Subtil © Helion & Company 2023)

Uesugi Kenshin Invades the Kantō

A more serious threat to the Hōjō had long been developing in the north in the form of the newly created Uesugi Kenshin, who made his first armed incursion into the Kantō on 11 July 1552. This small-scale raid was an important one, because it provided him with Numata Castle on the banks of the Tonegawa in Kōzuke. Numata would become Kenshin's jumping-off point for all his subsequent forays into the Kantō, but Kenshin withdrew from the field soon after the first raid because of illness.[20] In 1561 he returned and pushed his invasion as far as the walls of Odawara. It was the most decisive move made against Hōjō territories by anyone called Uesugi for many years and would be Kenshin's deepest penetration into the Kantō at any time. The Hōjō were however well-prepared for a possible attack of this sort, because there exists an undated letter from Hōjō Genan which refers to the vulnerability of Odawara Castle. Five hundred harquebuses are being sent to Odawara for its defence 'to prevent the enemy from getting any further than the edge of the moat'.[21] Umezawa suggests that the letter was written in 1561, so the supply of weapons may have taken place before Uesugi Kenshin's invasion.[22]

Kenshin's campaign began when he assembled his army at Numata. He then took Maebashi and pressed on to Odawara, beginning the siege from a base at Ōiso. Throughout this time the Tripartite Alliance held, and Shingen showed his support for Hōjō Ujiyasu by moving westwards into Kōzuke to threaten Kenshin's positions there. No relieving army ever materialised from Shingen's direction, but Kenshin was finally persuaded to withdraw from Odawara after 10 days because of surprise night attacks made on his siege lines by Hōjō *shinobi*. One of their raids led to the destruction by fire of Kenshin's baggage train. In addition, his men and horses were tired and there was a shortage of arrows, so Kenshin burned the town outside the walls and retreated.[23] His withdrawal was by no means ignominious, because after leaving Odawara Kenshin headed for Kamakura and had himself formally proclaimed as Kantō Kanrei at the Tsurugaoka Hachiman Shrine. The title had already been passed on to him by Yamanouchi Norimasa, but to have it announced in front of the shrine to Hachiman deep within Hōjō territory was a very symbolic act. Kenshin may not have captured Odawara, but to receive an accolade from the principal *kami* of the Kantō may have been his primary objective all along.

Later in that same year Kenshin advanced against the Takeda territories in Shinano province in an operation that provided the opening shots of what would develop into the epic yet indecisive Fourth Battle of Kawanakajima. Hōjō Ujiyasu stayed well clear of the action, and it would be several months before the three kingdoms again met in battle. The new site was Matsuyama Castle in Musashi, the location of the celebrated 'poetry battle', which had

---

20   *HGDK*, pp.292–294.

21   Udagawa 2013, pp.67–68.

22   Takuo Umezawa, *Matsuyama-jō kassen* (Matsuyama: Matsuyama Shobō, 2012), p.124.

23   *HK*, p.107.

remained a Uesugi possession since that time. It was very strong, being built on volcanic rock and was well supplied with ammunition, salt, beans, rice bran and straw for the horses.[24] The siege is interesting from several points of view. First, it would provide the only occasion when Hōjō Ujiyasu, Takeda Shingen and Uesugi Kenshin were involved at the same location, and it also appears to have been the first battle when the Hōjō can be assumed to be using firearms on a large scale.[25]

The defending commander Ōta Sanraku Sukemasa (1522–91) desperately needed to summon help from Uesugi Kenshin, and he did so in an unusual manner. As commander of both Matsuyama and Iwatsuki he had been instrumental in training a pack of dogs to act as messengers between the two places. Fifty dogs were based at Iwatsuki Castle and 50 at Matsuyama. They were trained to carry messages on slips of paper that were written in some form of invisible ink. The rolled-up slips of paper were placed into little bamboo tubes attached to the dogs' collars. The messenger dogs were released during the night and made their way back to Iwatsuki without arousing the suspicions of the besiegers. The paper was then placed in water and the message asking for help was revealed.[26]

Meanwhile Hōjō Ujimasa had requested aid from Takeda Shingen in a more conventional manner. His response was positive, and as well as sending reinforcements for the army miners were brought from the Takeda gold mines in Kai to tunnel into the hill on which Matsuyama was built. *Kanhasshū kosenroku* says that they were met by a hail of bullets from the defenders and many were killed, so labourers went out into nearby bamboo groves and bound up lengths of bamboo into bundles for the miners' protection from gunfire.[27] Their efforts were rewarded by the toppling of two wooden observation towers, but the digging had to be abandoned when they struck an underground stream and many of the excavators were drowned. Hōjō Tsunanari also tried setting fire to the castle using fire arrows, and one account of the siege adds that the attackers constructed some form of sow called a 'tortoise wagon' to provide a moveable protective roof when they approached the castle walls.[28]

Kōyō Gunkan includes an interesting anecdote relating to the siege of Matsuyama about two of Shingen's samurai and the value they placed upon personal honour. The incident involved one of Shingen's senior generals called Amari Haruyoshi (1534–64). Hikojirō, the son of his senior officer Yonekura Tango-no-Kami, was severely wounded when a bullet entered his abdomen and caused it to swell up from the accumulated blood. One of his attendants recalled an old folk remedy whereby the sufferer should drink diluted horse manure as a way of dispersing the blood, but the proud Hikojirō refused to comply, saying that he was going to die anyway and would not wish to disgrace

---

24 *HK*, pp.111–112.

25 Umezawa, p.41.

26 *KK*, pp.144–145.

27 *KK*, p.147.

28 Umezawa, p.126.

himself by drinking horse faeces. At this point Amari Haruyoshi intervened, telling Hikojirō's father that his son was too valuable a samurai to be allowed to die in this way. To encourage Hikojirō to take his medicine, Haruyoshi himself took the bucket of horse manure liquid and drank from it, adding that it tasted good! Convinced and greatly moved by his commander's example Hikojirō did the same. His wound healed and he lived to fight another day.[29]

Matsuyama eventually surrendered to the Hōjō/Takeda alliance on 5 May 1562. This was a profound disappointment for Kenshin, who was on his way to relieve the place at the head of a large army, so the frustrated Kenshin swung off to the east and turned his ire on to the Hōjō possession of Kisai Castle. Just as at Matsuyama the defenders 'were not in thrall to the gods of cowardice', but with only 50 horsemen in its garrison the castle fell after a day and a night of fierce fighting.[30] *Shinobi* may have been used because one account refers to trouble being caused by 'visitors without identification',[31] and *Kanhasshū kosenroku* credits a unit under Kenshin's general Honjō Echizen-no-Kami Shigenaga with advancing repeatedly up to the main gate, firing harquebuses and being greeted by equally fierce resistance.[32]

Uesugi Kenshin (1530–78) was one of the Hōjō's most relentless enemies. This statue of him stands in Yonezawa.

According to *Kanhasshū kosenroku* the castle fell because of an unnecessary panic among the defenders. The story relates that Kenshin was observing the castle bridge and saw reflected in the water the face of a woman wearing a plain white hemp kimono. The costume had a *mon* stencilled on it, so it was not an item that most women would have worn. Kenshin noticed this and so did Ōta Sukemasa. This person, they presumed, was one of the women and children held as hostages in the castle, so a group of bold Uesugi samurai forced their way through the marsh at the rear of the castle by using a raft. Soon they were inside the castle, where the sound of their war cries aroused terror among the captives held in the inner bailey, who became very alarmed and poured into the second bailey in a mistaken attempt at escape. When they reached the main gate the soldiers who were protecting it thought that the inner defences must have been destroyed by traitors. They panicked and abandoned their

---

29 Umezawa, p.103.

30 *HK*, p.112.

31 Akihiro Iwata, 'Sengoku shinobi wo ou', 2021, see <https://ranzan-shiseki.spec.ed.jp/wysiwyg/file/download/1/1223>, pp.18–20 (accessed 4 July 2022).

32 *KK*, p.154.

positions, so the castle soon fell without any further effort.[33] The Takeda's own chronicle *Kōyō Gunkan* adds a grisly detail missing from the Hōjō account to the effect that after the fall of Kisai Kenshin separated parents from their children and massacred at least 3,000 people.[34] After Kisai Kenshin marched into Shimotsuke and attacked the castles of Ōyama and Karasawayama. He then withdrew to Echigo.

The Second Battle of Kōnodai

Alliances in Sengoku Japan were notoriously fickle, and such a situation was one of the prompts that led to the Second Battle of Kōnodai, because certain minor retainers of the Hōjō (who are not named in the reference) abandoned their masters and submitted to Satomi Yoshihiro (?–1578), the son of the late Yoshitaka.[35] His army joined forces with Ōta Sukemasa on the heights of Kōnodai. The stage was set for a battle between Ujiyasu, the son of the victor of 1538, and the son of the loser at the same encounter.

Ujiyasu and Ujimasa left Odawara on 17 February 1564, and three days later set up camp on the right bank of the Ichikawa. This time they made no wide sweep upstream to engage the foe at Sagamidai. Instead the Hōjō army advanced straight up the slope on which Kōnodai sat, where they were greeted by a hail of arrows and a bombardment of dropped stones. Two samurai called Toyama Tanba-no-Kami Naokage and Tomonaga Masaie led the assault and both were killed, at which the Hōjō were successfully driven back across the river, just as the Prince of Oyumi should have done in 1538. Among the details that may be teased out from *Hōjō ki's* heroic descriptions of brave individual combat one notes the noise of battle from the clashing of *tsuba* (sword guards) and the sound of the harquebuses reverberating between the mountain and the river as the Hōjō attacked into the face of gunfire, although the firing was curtailed when rain started falling.[36] *Kanhasshū kosenroku* also refers to guns being used against the Hōjō at Kōnodai to drive back their assault up the slope leading to the castle.[37]

Satomi Yoshihiro was exultant at having succeeded where his father had failed, and that night the castle of Kōnodai was the scene of much celebration. Two brave Hōjō *shinobi* reported this back to Ujiyasu, who decided that the plans he had already set in motion would sweep away the exhausted and overconfident garrison in the morning. Unknown to the Satomi, while the main body of the Hōjō were pulling back across the river in apparent defeat, a detachment under Ujimasa had begun moving in a wide semi-circle to take up a position at their rear. Rain and mist concealed their movements, and

---

33 *KK*, p.154.

34 Umezawa, pp.104–105.

35 J. M. Dixon, 'Kōnodai and its spots of interest', *Transactions of the Asiatic Society of Japan* 10, 1881, p.44.

36 *HK*, pp.116–117.

37 *KK*, p.169.

when dawn broke the bleary-eyed Satomi troops found themselves being attacked from all sides as flags appeared out of the shadows of the forest. One account suggests that the Satomi were so surprised that some of them ran out of the castle without any armour. The Hōjō were again victorious, and once more a leader of the Satomi fled precipitously from a battlefield at Kōnodai.

The Hōjō and Satomi forces square off against each other, with Mount Fuji looming in the distance.

Satomi Yoshihiro's son, however, was not so fortunate. The boy's name was Hirotsugu and he was fighting in his first battle at the age of 15. Hirotsugu was challenged and killed by Matsuda Yasuyoshi of the Hōjō, who was filled with remorse when he realised that he had been responsible for the death of a child. In an episode similar to the tale of the killing of Taira Atsumori at the battle of Ichinotani in 1184 (from which the passage in *Hōjō Godai ki* may well have been lifted), Matsuda quits the battlefield to become a monk and spends the rest of his life praying for the soul of Hirotsugu.[38] With the castle secure, Hōjō Ujiyasu sat down on his camp stool and expressed his own emotions through poetry, using references to the present battlefield and the location of the fugitive Satomi lord whom he wished to pursue:

Conquering the foe as I wished at Kōnodai/
Now do I behold the evening sunshine at Katsuura.[39]

An interesting anecdote from the battle of Kōnodai concerns the piece of armour known as a *nodowa* or throat-ring, which hung below the chin to provide protection at the top of the body armour. Ōta Sukemasa had been wounded twice when Shimizu Tarōza'emon, who was noted for his strength, threw him to the ground and tried to cut off his head. He was having problems

38 Turnbull, *The Samurai Art of War*, p.108.
39 Dixon, p.45.

Hōjō Ujimasa goes into action at the second battle of Kōnodai,
accompanied by a samurai bearing the Hōjō *mon* on his *sashimono*.

doing this, so Sukemasa explained helpfully that he was wearing a *nodowa*, which his assailant would first have to remove. Tarōzaèmon bowed in respect, and thanked Sukemasa for the information, promising him that he would now die a noble death. But just as he was about to remove the *nodowa* two young followers of Sukemasa rushed up and threw Tarōzaèmon to the ground, so Sukemasa decapitated him instead.[40] Curiously, other stories about a strong man of the Hōjō called Shimizu Tarōzaèmon make no mention of this incident and have him living to a ripe old age.

The Siege of Ikewada

Following his victory at Kōnodai Ujiyasu pressed on into Shimōsa province, but he was never able to eliminate the Satomi even though an important Hōjō victory was gained on the Bōsō peninsula in 1565 when Ujiyasu captured Ikewada Castle in Kazusa.[41] To the west, south and north of the castle were vast deep paddy fields, while a mountain stood on its eastern side. Ujiyasu ordered his army to climb the mountain to attack, and on descending his troops tore down the commoners' houses for material to make fascines along with grass, bamboo and even broken arrows. The resulting bundles were tipped into the castle's dry moat. Arrows and bullets 'poured down like rain from above' as the Hōjō troops crossed the makeshift causeway, but this provided no hindrance for the attackers, who trampled over the dead bodies of their comrades to carry out their assault.[42] *Bōsō Satomi Gunki* states that matters were resolved when one of the defenders who had a grudge against his master set fire to a tower at midnight.[43] There is also a sad piece of local folklore which says that the women of the castle fled, but when they heard the sound of the wind blowing through the maize fields they thought it was the noise of pursuing enemies and committed suicide. From then until the Meiji Period the local people would not grow maize.[44]

In true *gunkimono* style however, *Hōjō Godai ki* concentrates instead on an episode of individual samurai heroism, because at Ikewada three men were involved in killing one prestigious enemy named as Tagaya Hyōenosuke. The Hōjō men are identified as Date Echizen-no-Kami, Nakayama Zaèmonnojō and Kataoka Heijibei. Even at this late stage in samurai history when most warriors wielded spears from horseback, prowess at *kyūba no michi* (the way of bow and horse) was still highly valued, or at least that is what the chronicler wants his readers to think! In the illustrated version of *Hōjō Godai ki* Date and Nakayama are loosing bows from opposite sides of their victim, while Kataoka runs up with his sword already drawn to take the head. Clearly, all

---

40 *KK*, p.175.

41 *HGDK*, pp.322–325.

42 *KK*, p.196.

43 Bōsō Shōso Kankō Kai, p.389.

44 Guide to Ikewada Castle, <http://umoretakojo.jp/Shiro/Kantou/Chiba/Ikewada/index.htm> (accessed 8 May 2022).

At the battle of Ikewada in 1565 three samurai took part in the killing of a distinguished enemy. There was then an investigation over whose contribution had been the most valuable.

three played a part in Hyōenosuke's death, but Ujiyasu had to decide whose action was most important and then reward the three accordingly.

The three men concerned knelt in front of their commander with their helmets at their sides. *Hōjō Godai ki* goes into great detail over the evidence based on the testimony of the two eyewitnesses, and the questions posed. What colour armour was so-and-so wearing? Who loosed the deadly arrow? Ujiyasu considered the arguments and reached his conclusion. The accolade of *ichiban* ('number one') went to Date Echizen-no-Kami, whose arrow was responsible for bringing the victim down. *Niban* (second place) was awarded to Nakayama Za'emonnojō for attacking a fierce enemy on his bow-hand side, from where the assailant would be particularly vulnerable to an arrow loosed against him in return. In third place was Kataoka Heijibei, the man who actually took Hyōenosuke's head. In Ujiyasu's eyes the head-taking was the easiest task of the three and involved less risk, but it poses an interesting reflection on the high value that is usually credited to the collecting of heads by samurai.[45]

---

45   *HGDK*, pp.322–325; Turnbull, *The Samurai Art of War*, pp.110–113.

7

Hōjō Ujiyasu's Later Years

Hōjō Ujiyasu's long and unremitting military career was carried out to a background of gains and losses, a situation encapsulated in the story of the 10 battles of Karasawayama Castle in Shimotsuke province. The identification of 10 separate sieges is somewhat forced, as are the dates allotted to them, but the sequence of events provides a fascinating summary of the interplay between warfare and personality in Sengoku Japan.

The huge sprawling *yamashiro* (mountain castle) of Karasawayama (which appears is some accounts under the name of Sano Castle) was owned by the Sano family, who claimed descent from Fujiwara Hidesato, the hero who had quelled the rebellion of Taira Masakado in the year 940. Proud of both his pedigree and his independence, its current lord Sano Masatsuna (1529–74) maintained a delicate balancing act between the favours of Uesugi Kenshin and Hōjō Ujiyasu, both of whom coveted Masatsuna's support because of Karasawayama's strategic location on the route from Kenshin's Maebashi Castle in Kōzuke to Koga in the heart of the Kantō. It thus controlled communications right through the vulnerable border area.

Sano Masatsuna had succeeded to the family headship in 1559, and from then onwards Karasawayama would experience a series of attacks either by Kenshin or by Ujiyasu. Karasawayama's repeated resistance gave the castle the reputation of being the best defended *yamashiro* in the Kantō, although in most instances serious bloodshed was avoided because Sano Masatsuna would surrender to the besieger, only to revolt again in favour of the other side when the current victor withdrew his army to deal with a new threat from elsewhere.

The first siege of Karasawayama is supposed to have been conducted by Hōjō Ujimasa in 1559. It has passed into legend because of an anecdote in *Kanhasshū kosenroku* whereby Kenshin used bold psychological warfare to disperse the Hōjō. Wearing a white priestly robe and no armour, and with a flag bearer in attendance carrying a banner on which was inscribed the single ideograph *mu* ('nothingness'), Kenshin rode silently up to the castle gate. The Hōjō besiegers were astonished and none dared approach him, thinking the apparition to be an avatar of the warrior deity Bishamon-ten. Ujimasa accordingly withdrew his army and the first siege of Karasawayama came to an end.[1]

A second, and better authenticated, siege followed in 1561 when the Uesugi army abandoned their siege of Odawara. A triumphant Ujiyasu went on the offensive and surrounded Karasawayama Castle while Kenshin was otherwise engaged fighting the Fourth Battle of Kawanakajima. Having no outside help this time Masatsuna surrendered to the Hōjō, which Kenshin regarded as a betrayal. He therefore attacked Karasawayama a year later in 1562 but was repulsed by the now pro-Hōjō Sano. The fourth siege happened when Kenshin failed to relieve Matsuyama, as was discussed above. He went on the rampage and took several castles in the Kantō including Karasawayama, which surrendered without a fight.

Sano Masatsuna declared for the Hōjō again when Kenshin left Shimotsuke, so a fifth battle of Karasawayama occurred during the second lunar month of 1564 when the Uesugi returned in force and mounted the fiercest attack out of all the 10 episodes. The castle had good water supplies and held out, even though the Hōjō were busy fighting the Second Battle of Kōnodai and were unable to send help. When he realised this Kenshin returned in strength, and Masatsuna finally surrendered peacefully to Kenshin following the entreaties of Sano's allies Satake Yoshishige and Utsunomiya Hirotsuna. One of the outcomes of the negotiated surrender was that Masatsuna gave his son for adoption by Kenshin.

The sixth round at Karasawayama happened later that same year while Kenshin was fighting the Fifth Battle of Kawanakajima. This episode is included in *Hōjō ki* and *Kanhasshū kosenroku*, and began with Hōjō Ujimasa capturing Gion (Ōyama) Castle in Shimotsuke. The attack on Gion lasted three days and three nights, with a prominent role being played by Hōjō Tsunanari 'on a fleet horse with his yellow Hachiman flag … One hundred Ōyama horsemen tried to hold him back and over ten of them were killed by his arrows.'[2] Ujimasa's subsequent attack on Karasawayama provides some clues to its defences that are not recorded elsewhere because 'from the mountain top large stones and great tree trunks were thrown down', while 'men and horses died in the intense heat and their provisions ran out'.[3] Facing a long stay in the lines Ujimasa abandoned camp and returned to Odawara late in the seventh lunar month. *Karasawa-jō rōdanki*, an undated chronicle of the Sano family, includes some more interesting factual material about how the Sano domain was defended around this time:

> In order to prevent hostile incursions, a fort was set up on the border and a guard post was established there. The locals who manned it received a stipend of either 10 or 15 *kan* and were known as the Kyō-ikki ['The Local League']. In addition they supplied ashigaru archers who received 2 or 3 *kan* each. The people from five or seven villages around were in charge of the guard post. The locals had to hurry

---

1   *KK*, pp.111–113.

2   *HK*, p.125; *KK*, p.202.

3   *KK*, p.204.

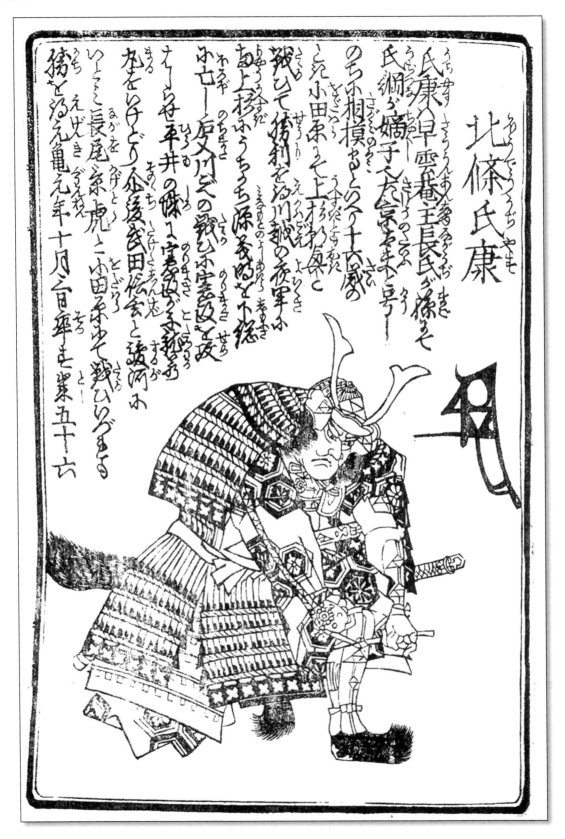

北條氏康

氏康は早雲庵主長氏が孫そ
氏綱が嫡子ぞ七寸五分また号一
のち不相模をところ十六歳の
とき小田原にそ上け初陣て
戦ひて勝利をぬ川越の夜軍か
あ上挙ふうちに源義ゆと不慮
わ亡一庚文川ぐの戦ひ宇宙ぶ及
たーうせ平井の條入宇宙ぶ及
卆をらず企後武田仪会と援河の
いとく長尾糸虎二小田原また戦ひりづまる
豬をとる元亀元年十月三日卆まも素五十六

and gather at the guard post when they heard the sound of the bell or the conch shell. At the same time, when the bell or conch sounded in the villages the *yoriki* [samurai horsemen] and the ashigaru archers were supposed to gather at the main castle. In addition, various signals were agreed so that when a battle began the women and children knew where to go and supplies could be transported.[4]

Facing page: Hōjō Ujiyasu fastens the cords of his *suneate* (shinguards) before going into battle.

In 1566 Masatsuna declared for the Hōjō again and faced an attack by Kenshin in early 1567 that was broken off because of severe winter weather conditions. Later that same year a thaw occurred and Karasawayama surrendered to Kenshin in what is counted as his eighth operation against the castle. By 1570 Masatsuna had joined the Hōjō again so Kenshin mounted a ninth siege in the winter that also had to be abandoned.

Sano Masatsuna died in 1574 and was succeeded by his son Munetsuna, who faced a tenth and final attack from Uesugi Kenshin in 1577, but Kenshin was driven off and would die the following year. Sano Munetsuna was noted for his support for the new technology of firearms, encouraging their production and urging his subordinates to deploy them in battle. Ironically, he would be shot off his horse and killed at the battle of Suhanazaka in 1585.[5] His death threw the clan into confusion, so Hōjō Ujimasa sent his brother Ujitada (1556–93) to be the adopted heir of the Sano, and Karasawayama stayed within the Hōjō's sphere of influence until Hideyoshi's invasion in 1590.

The Sano family's behaviour at Karasawayama is an extreme example of a situation typical of the era. As an old-style *sengoku daimyō* with a modest landholding facing the powers of the new 'super-daimyo' he could only survive in the face of leaders of the stature of Ujiyasu by making alliances with them. What is extraordinary is the way he shifted allegiances and yet still survived. It is amazing that Kenshin allowed Sano Masatsuna to escape with his head still on his shoulders and his control of the castle intact until the next round of disloyalty.

The Siege of Usui

Uesugi Kenshin moved directly against the Hōjō in 1566. He advanced first into Shimotsuke and went on into Hitachi to take Oda. He then marched into Shimōsa and secured Funabashi, an important river port for Edo Bay and a useful base for transporting supplies. Kenshin's next target was Usui Castle in Shimōsa. The castellan was Hara Tanesada (1507–69), a retainer of the Chiba family who were vassals of the Hōjō. Tanesada defended his castle desperately against the Uesugi force with 200 horsemen under his command. Kenshin's army got as far as the inner moat and the castle seemed likely to fall because Ujiyasu was unable to send reinforcements in time, but then *Hōjō ki* introduces us to Matsuda Magotarō Yasusato (1540–1609) one of the leading Hōjō samurai at the battle. The author 'dresses the warrior' in traditional style:

---

4   A chronicle of Karasawa <http://muromachi.movie.coocan.jp/karasawa/karasawa01.html> (accessed 9 May 2022).

5   *HK*, p.200.

Matsuda Magotarō Yasusato had under his command 150 *dōshin* [samurai]. He cut his way through both the first and second ranks of the enemy and advanced as far as Kenshin's *hatamoto*. That day Magotarō wore a Takatsuno armour. It was a red suit of armour ornamented with golden lions. He rode a black horse and wielded a large *naginata* in the 'eight sides' style of sword fighting. He thrust its blade into the *yoriki* and cut down eight men. After that he gave it to a servant to hold and took an oak shafted *bō* and knocked other men off their horses. Among the heads he took were those of Kageyama Shinshirō and one called Hashimoto, who were both great names. The Echigo force withdrew when the sun set.[6]

The fighting resumed the following morning, and once again Matsuda Magotarō took a prominent part, which greatly impressed Kenshin and led him to make an approving comment. He said that Magotarō resembled the red devils who were said to live in Iwafuneyama, a holy mountain in his territory. From that time on Magotarō was known to the Hōjō as as 'Devil Magotarō' or 'The Red Devil of Matsuda' – and would be richly rewarded by Ujiyasu.[7]

According to the chronicler the Red Devil's individual samurai prowess inspired a successful sortie out of the castle that turned the tide of battle. The Uesugi army withdrew to their lines, intending to attack the following day, but when the time came Usui Castle was eerily silent. This was probably due to Hara Tanesada's practice of performing divination, which must have indicated to him that it was an inauspicious day to fight. The silence unsettled Kenshin, who withdrew his forces from Usui. That may have been a sensible decision, but it was a humiliating reversal for the great warlord. His failure to capture Usui meant that his gains in neighbouring Kōzuke, Shimotsuke and Hitachi were isolated with poor communications between them, a state of affairs that ultimately forced him to accept a truce with Hōjō Ujiyasu.[8]

The Hōjō and Takeda Shingen

The latter years of the 1560s saw renewed fighting between the Hōjō and the Takeda after the collapse of their earlier alliance following the ruin of the Imagawa family at the battle of Okehazama in 1560. As is well known, Imagawa Yoshimoto set out at the head of a huge army with the aim of advancing on Kyoto. He was stopped in Owari province by the then minor daimyo Oda Nobunaga, who defeated and killed Yoshimoto. Yoshimoto's son Ujizane (1538–1615) inherited the clan leadership. His mother was Takeda Shingen's sister and his wife was Hōjō Ujiyasu's daughter: two valuable links had contributed to the Tripartite Alliance between the three families, but when the Imagawa suffered the disaster of Okehazama Suruga was up for grabs and their vassals and allies started to desert them. Takeda Shingen was the first to appreciate the opportunity and planned to annex Suruga for himself. He was

---

6   *HK*, p.123; with a similar account in *KK*, p.192.

7   *HK*, p.123.

8   *HK*, p.124.

opposed in this by his son Yoshinobu – the one married into the Imagawa family – but in a separate development Shingen accused Yoshinobu of treason and had him imprisoned. Shingen then annulled the marriage, so Imagawa Ujizane turned to the Hōjō for support and also courted Uesugi Kenshin.

Shingen's invasion of Suruga began in December 1568. Imagawa Ujizane tried to ambush the Takeda army, but so many of his supposed allies had deserted him that Shingen was able to destroy the Imagawa headquarters of Sunpu. Ujizane fled to Kakegawa Castle in Tōtōmi, but instead of finding refuge there he was subjected to an attack by Tokugawa Ieyasu, to whom Takeda Shingen had promised a share of Imagawa territory in return for his support. Meanwhile Shingen built Kuno Castle to be his base in Suruga in place of Sunpu, and it was at this point that the Hōjō intervened on the Imagawa's behalf. Ujiyasu sent a relief army to the Satta Pass, but all that happened was a standoff with the Takeda forces in the vicinity. With no relief in sight Imagawa Ujizane surrendered Kakegawa Castle on 17 May 1569, which effectively gave notice of the end of the Imagawa as a serious force. Ujizane took refuge with the Hōjō at Tokura Castle in Izu province and later moved to Odawara, where he waited for the Takeda to attack again.

According to *Hōjō ki*, Shingen's next advance into Suruga was accompanied by an act of desecration comparable to the Satomi's attack on Kamakura in 1526. Certain elements within Shingen's vanguard plundered the Great Shrine of Mishima Daimyōjin, which lay just inside Hōjō territory in Izu province. Divine retribution followed, just as had happened at Kamakura, but in this instance the *kami's* revenge came when the Takeda were still in camp:

> Towards evening on the 19th day black clouds gathered and rain started falling from the direction of the Hakone Mountains. As night fell a fierce wind blew and great rain fell; the falling rain acted like a veritable washbowl. A huge volume of water advanced towards the camp and soon it was up to their waists. Our own vanguard had climbed to higher ground, from which nothing could now be heard. They were shocked and thought, 'This is not normal. It is the sound of Mishima Myōjin.'[9]

The Takeda encampment is likely to have been a substantial affair with temporary wooden buildings and bamboo fences, so the flood water would have caused great devastation, taking everything away including huts, supplies, weapons and equipment.[10]

The heavenly punishment at Mishima may have been one of the prompts that propelled Shingen towards the grandiose operation that would provide Hōjō Ujiyasu with the last major challenge of his reign. In a bold move that has echoes of Kenshin's march in the same direction in 1561, Shingen attacked Odawara Castle in 1569. What is remarkable about Shingen's attempt is the direction of advance that he chose: not from newly occupied friendly Suruga but straight across the enemy territory of Musashi.

---

9   *HK*, p.133.

10   *HK*, p.134.

This print by Yoshitoshi shows Uesugi Kenshin contemplating the moon. He is wearing a monk's head cowl.

Hōjō Ujikuni (1541–97) was Ujimasa's brother, who successfully defended Hachigata Castle against Takeda Shingen in 1569. In 1590 he remained at Hachigata to defend it against Hideyoshi but was forced to surrender. This is an edited detail from a print by Kuniyoshi.

Above: The reconstructed gate of Hachigata Castle in Hachigata Castle Museum, as shown from the inside. It has an open firing platform.

On 10 October 1569 Shingen's army began the campaign by laying siege to Hachigata Castle, which was defended by Ujiyas's third son Ujikuni (1541–97). He drove the Takeda away from the castle, but the besiegers merely continued their advance and moved on to Takiyama. Takiyama was held by Ujikuni's brother Ujiteru, who also repulsed Shingen's attack. To carry on from there to the Hōjō capital of Odawara with two intact fortresses behind him was a surprising decision for the experienced Takeda Shingen. Odawara was very well defended, and it is during the subsequent siege that *Kanhasshū kosenroku* provides the first unambiguous mention in any of the chronicles of large-scale harquebus use by the Hōjō. As confirmed by the Genan letter noted above, Odawara was defended using possibly 500 firearms. When Shingen arrived the Miura-*shū* (Miura company) sallied out to do some fighting against the Takeda but prudently pulled back. After that not a single soldier went out of the castle, but from time to time arrows and bullets were discharged from loopholes in the towers.[11] The situation in Odawara was serious. The number of people within the castle had been swelled by farmers and others moving in for safety when a siege seemed imminent, and the

---

11 *KK*, p.226.

pressure of numbers threatened to stretch the garrison's resources to their limits. Fortunately, Shingen was dissuaded from pursuing an assault by the strength of Odawara's walls, so this second siege of the castle only lasted three days, after which on 9 November Shingen burned the castle town outside and withdrew, just as Kenshin had done eight years earlier.

Hōjō Ujiyasu quickly realised that he had been given an excellent opportunity for a decisive showdown with the Takeda. He also appreciated that this would have to be done in the mountains if the Hōjō were not to face the famous Takeda cavalry on the flat plains beyond, so his plan was for Ujiteru and Ujikuni to ambush the Takeda as they made their way home through the pass of Mimasetoge. This was carried out meticulously on 15 November, and during the ensuing battle Asari Nobutane of the Takeda was hit in the breast by a stray bullet and killed.[12] The ambush almost succeeded in defeating the Takeda but, after a day of fighting, Yamagata Masakage, one of the Takeda's most experienced generals, launched a devastating flank attack on the Hōjō left wing. The main body of the Takeda then broke through and escaped.

Takeda Shingen left Kai for a third invasion of Suruga on 2 January 1570. The Hōjō had clearly anticipated such a move, because sometime during the previous September Hōjō Ujimasa sent orders to Fuse Sado-no-Kami, who had the responsibility of defending Kanbara Castle in Suruga, to prepare for a Takeda incursion. It was noted that Fuse had assembled 20 *yoriki* in the castle together with an unspecified number of archers and harquebusiers.[13] Kanbara eventually came under attack from a division of Shingen's army that was led by his son Katsuyori (1546–82). During the night of 11 January Katsuyori's army set fire to the outlying buildings that constituted Kanbara's rudimentary castle town. He then launched a massive attack on the castle, killing Hōjō Tsunashige, the second son of Ujiyasu's uncle Hōjō Genan along with his younger brother. According to *Hōjō ki*, Tsunashige's angry ghost would remain to haunt the castle hill, and his unhappy spirit terrified the local people for many years to come.[14]

When the Hōjō lost Kanbara their influence in Suruga greatly declined. By comparison, the defeat caused nothing but panic among the Imagawa, who were thrown into further turmoil when the Takeda continued westwards along the Tōkaidō and captured Hanazawa Castle. Takeda Shingen was well on the way to achieving mastery of Suruga with its immediate access to the sea. So far all the major losses had been suffered by the Imagawa, but as the year wore on certain long-standing fortresses of the Hōjō in the Suruga/Izu border area also became targets. One probing raid by the Takeda in September took them as far as the key Hōjō base of Nirayama. A few days later Kōkokuji, the castle once given to Hōjō Sōun, managed to hold out under a Hōjō retainer named Haga Ujitsugu before the Takeda army returned to Kōfu.[15]

---

12 *KK*, p.228.

13 Udagawa 2013, p.57.

14 *HK*, pp.142–143.

15 Haga Ujitsugu was a valued retainer, as shown by the fact that he was the only one to be allowed to use the character 'Uji' in his given name.

During this raid another Takeda division threatened Fukazawa Castle, which lay to the north-west of Odawara. Its location near the border with Sagami made it an ideal base should Shingen ever contemplate another move against the Hōjō capital, so a unit of his army returned to lay siege to Fukazawa on 28 January 1571. It was held by the redoubtable Hōjō Tsunanari, who considered a peaceful surrender because of an arrow letter delivered to him over the castle wall. The letter was from Shingen and was conciliatory in tone, reminding Tsunanari and Ujiyasu of the clans' previous happy alliance, and how the Takeda had supported him when Odawara had been attacked by the Uesugi in 1561. Shingen also suggested that the Hōjō's current agreement with the Imagawa was only due to the machinations of Kenshin and that harmony should be restored between them. Tsunanari may have been tempted, but instead of surrendering he held out defiantly for two further months. Shingen then brought up miners from Kai who tunnelled under the walls, and when gaping holes appeared in his physical defences Tsunanari submitted honourably and withdrew to Tamanawa with Ujiyasu's blessing. With this act the Takeda control of Suruga was confirmed and Hōjō Ujiyasu had to accept that his ancient western borders still marked the limits of Hōjō influence in that direction.

The fall of Fukazawa was also accompanied by a sadly symbolic loss for the Hōjō. Tsunanari had always been devoted to the *kami* Hachiman, and prayed to him with sacred ablutions on the fifteenth day of every month. As commander of the Hōjō's Yellow Regiment who bore the Hōjō *mon* on a yellow background on their flags, Tsunanari cherished a striking personal war banner that had the same yellow field but bore the two characters that spelled out Hachiman's name. When Fukazawa surrendered this so-called 'Yellow Hachiman Flag' was taken as a trophy. Shingen however took great pains not to ridicule the brave Tsunanari in any way, and instead gave the flag to Sanada Nobutada (1547–1632).[16]

The Administration of the Domain Under Ujiyasu

Hōjō Ujiyasu was a wise administrator of the ever-expanding Hōjō domain, and under his tutelage the satellite castle system evolved from being a purely defensive network into an administrative tool for governing the newly pacified territories. Finance was also brought under control, and in 1559 he standardised the amount of tax that any retainer could take from his own land, which determined that retainer's military obligation to the Hōjō. The results appeared in the form of the *Odawara-shū shoryō yakuchō*, the 'Domesday Book' of the Hōjō domain. For the first time Ujiyasu knew exactly what his

---

16 Jōzan Yuasa, *Jōzan Kidan*, c. 1853, 1912 reprint, pp.87–88. <https://archive.org/details/jozankidan00yuasuoft/page/n1> (accessed 22 July 2019). Copies would be made and flown whenever the Yellow Regiment went into future battles. The original flag from Fukazawa is preserved in the Sanada Museum at Matsushiro in Nagano Prefecture.

domain was worth, a momentous step towards the Hōjō taking control of the means of production within their boundaries.

The administrators who oversaw village affairs often wore another hat: that of the loyal samurai who would lead the villagers into battle, so we read of village headmen being granted tax exemptions if they became vassals of the Hōjō and led a *shū* (military unit), and even being granted a stipend in return for their own military service. The advantage for the daimyo was that he acquired more names on his 'retained' list in the lower reaches of the samurai class in return for very little outlay. The village headmen benefited by enjoying the enhanced social status that valiant service could only further improve. Such enthusiasts would maintain lists of able-bodied men who would be willing to put down their tools, pick up a spear and follow their swaggering local leaders into battle.

One other development that greatly increased the control the Hōjō exercised over the men who owned and farmed the land was the gradual separation of the Hōjō warriors from their ancestral localities, because the particular area of land that sustained a samurai was often to be found a distance away from the castle where he was stationed. The identification of a samurai with a village – a hallmark of medieval society going back many generations – was becoming blurred. The total separation of the military and the agricultural function may have been many decades away, but its beginnings lay in the daimyo's need for control of the domain, and this the Hōjō realised very early on in their rise to power.

By the time of Ujiyasu's death late in 1571 his clan had risen in status of from that of a small ambitious *sengoku daimyō* to being lord of one of the Three Kingdoms who embraced modern military technology. As further evidence for the latter, there is an order from Ujiyasu of 17 March 1571 commanded a certain Kondō Manei to send harquebuses and bullets to the Edo-*shū* to prepare for an impending attack on Edo by the Satomi. What is interesting about this document is that it is addressed not to a castle owner but to a blacksmith in Edo's Asakusa district who normally made ship's anchors. The context therefore suggests that he has become a gunsmith, so one may conclude that harquebuses and bullets were being manufactured within the Hōjō domain by 1571.[17] The Hōjō military revolution was now well established.

---

17   Udagawa 2013, p.59.

8

Ujimasa and the Hōjō's Fragile Borders

The fourth daimyō, Hōjō Ujimasa (1538–90) lived through the notable victories of Oda Nobunaga but then had to confront Hideyoshi.

The great Hōjō Ujiyasu died at Odawara Castle on 21 October 1571. Ujimasa had reigned officially as daimyo for the last 11 years of his illustrious father's life, but he was now on his own. Fortunately for the Hōjō Ujimasa was prudent as well as brave, and very soon he wisely concluded a peace agreement with Takeda Shingen. This meant that the Hōjō's borders with the Takeda-controlled province of Suruga were secure once again, but the alliance promised even greater advantages for the Takeda because the new arrangements allowed Shingen to confront major challenges in the west without any fear of a rear attack from the Hōjō. The result was the operation that culminated in his great victory over Tokugawa Ieyasu early in 1573 at the battle of Mikata-ga-Hara. It is not generally known that as part of their alliance Hōjō Ujimasa supplied 2,000 troops towards the Takeda war effort at Mikata-ga-Hara, among whom was their 'strong man' Shimizu Tarōza'emon, who is said to have torn a man's head off using only his bare hands.[1]

Takeda Shingen died unexpectedly later that same year, felled by a sniper's bullet during the siege of Noda Castle, and Uesugi Kenshin would follow Shingen to the 'White Jade Pavilion' within five years. The confusion within the two families during this time of great upheaval meant that some pressure was taken off the Hōjō, so Ujimasa exercised the freedom to expand into Kōzuke and even into Shinano. Otherwise he and his son Ujinao spent most of the time defending their fragile eastern borders with Hitachi against the Satake, their western borders against Shingen's heir Takeda Katsuyori and the sea coast against the Satomi.

---

1   Turnbull, *The Samurai Art of War*, p.151.

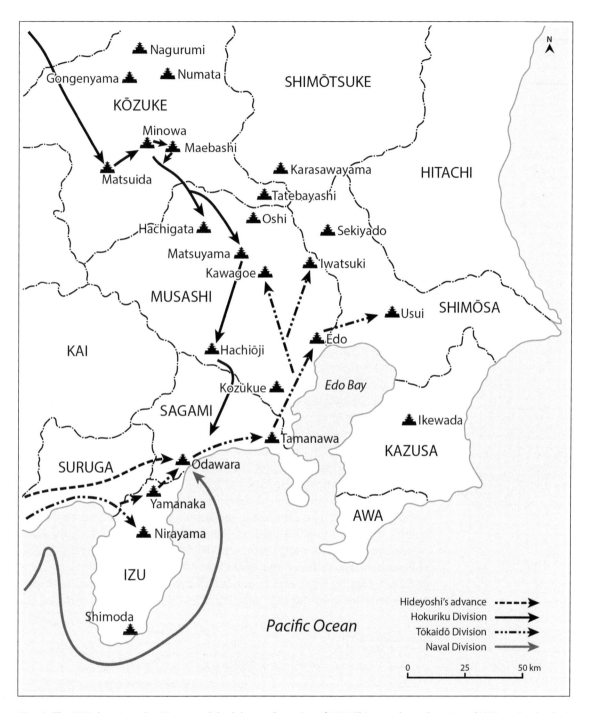

Map 2. The Hōjō domain under Ujimasa and the Odawara Campaign of 1590. This map shows the principal Hōjō castles that had been established by the time of Hideyoshi's invasion in 1590. His forces marched against the Hōjō in two main divisions. The Tōkaidō Division moved along the Pacific Ocean coastline followed by Hideyoshi's main body of troops. The Hokurikudō Division invaded the Kantō from the north, while the naval detachment blockaded Odawara. The main satellite castles and the associated engagements are shown.

Ujimasa and Firearms

The reign of Ujimasa takes the Hōjō story up to the time when Hideyoshi invaded in 1590, and as his era progresses we note further developments in military technology, particularly through the development of firearms and their deployment in castles. By 1579 there is evidence that Ujimasa is using organised harquebus squads at Hiroki Castle, because he 'lined up his archers and harquebusiers in strict ranks'.[2] A few years later at Hachigata Castle, of the 13 harquebusiers listed for 1583 under the name of Chichibu Magojirō, three were retained as part of his main troop while the other 10 were assigned to a specialist firearms unit called the Akiyama-shū.[3] Finally, conclusive proof for the existence of firearms squads among the Hōjō by 1584 at the very latest is provided on 18 December of that year when Ujimasa grants a stipend for maintaining a 10 man-strong harquebus squad to Utsuki Shimōsa-no-Kami Ujihisa.[4] An incident during that same year illustrates how many harquebuses could now be deployed in a typical battle, because an extensive anti-Hōjō alliance led by Satake Yoshishige confronted Ujimasa in a three-month standoff at the undistinguished flat plain of Numajiri. Records show that the Satake *hatamoto* fielded 1,000 harquebuses, while the Satake unit from the eastern districts of their home province placed 1,100 on the battlefield. Theirs is the largest number noted in the coalition; most supplied between 50 and 100 harquebuses while a unit identified only as Yamada contributed 20. If an overall tally is made across the whole anti-Hōjō alliance of 39 names, the number of harquebuses that could theoretically be brought into action against the Hōjō by the Satake in 1584 is a staggering 8,680.[5]

Similar numbers of firearms in individual armies now begin to be noticed throughout Japan. In that same year of 1584 down in Kyushu, Ryūzōji Takanobu, whose tactical layout the Portuguese Jesuit Luis Frois compared to a European army, was estimated as having 1,000 harquebuses in his front ranks at the battle of Okita-Nawate.[6] Three years later in 1587 Hideyoshi invaded Kyushu and his general Miyabe Keishin used 1,000 harquebuses from behind field defences at the battle of Nejirozaka.[7] Even Kumabe Chikanaga, a minor landowner from Higo province who rebelled against the new daimyo Hideyoshi had placed over him, could field 740 harquebuses at Jōmura Castle in 1587.[8] Finally, when the humiliated Shimazu were required to supply troops for Hideyoshi's Korean expedition in 1592 their orders included the

---

2   *KK*, p.286.

3   *Shinpen Saitama-ken shi*, Saitama Prefecture, *Shinpen Saitama-ken shi. Shiryō-hen 6: Chūsei 2: Komonjo 2 Sengoku* (Saitama: Saitama-ken, 1980), p.294. Henceforward *SSKS*.

4   Udagawa 2007, pp.32, 176.

5   Hitachi-Ōta City, *Hitachi-Ōta shi shi* (Hitachi-Ōta City: Hitachi-Ōta Publications 1979), pp.358–359

6   Kiichi Matsuda and Momota Kawasaki (transl.), *Kanyaku Furoisu Nihon shi*, vol. 10 (Tokyo: Chūōkōron-Shinsha, 2000), p.278.

7   Masaya Suzuki, *Teppō to Nihonjin* (Tokyo: Chikuma Shobō, 2000), pp.152–153.

8   Eishi Araki, *Higo kunishū ikki* (Kumamoto: Shuppan Bunka Kaikan, 2012), p.57.

supply of 1,500 harquebuses.[9] It therefore seems reasonable to conclude that for period 1584–1592 most individual daimyo were able to commit between 1,000 and 2,000 harquebuses to a battle situation, and a combination of allied effort could yield a much higher level of firepower. The Hōjō were no different; when Hideyoshi surrounded Odawara Castle in 1590 three harquebuses were stationed at every loophole in the castle walls with one *ōdeppō* (large-calibre harquebus) in between them.[10]

The Satake Wars

The Hōjō's main enemies to the east of their domains between 1570 and 1590 were the Satake family of Hitachi under Satake Yoshishige (1547–1612) and his son Yoshinobu (1570–1633). On the edge of the Hōjō territories lay a long narrow strip of Shimōsa province: a flat, unwelcoming area of meandering rivers and swamps where the borders of four provinces lay very close together. The strategy on both sides was that of establishing forward positions and garrisoning them against the inevitable counter-attacks. These stubborn little outposts were simple forts at the bottom of the satellite castle hierarchy where discipline and vigilance were strictly imposed, as shown by the surviving regulations for the Hōjō's Hamaiba Castle, a similar structure built in the Hakone Mountains against the Takeda:

> The garrison are forbidden to go out west of the castle; collecting vegetation is limited to the east side of the castle.
>
> Human faeces and horse manure must be removed from the castle every day and disposed of beyond the distance of one bowshot.
>
> It is strictly forbidden for anyone on duty to leave the castle for unauthorised reasons. If the man on duty enters the mountains for the purpose of hunting deer or raccoon dogs he will be executed and the man in charge of him will be severely punished.
>
> Guard duty must be maintained in the towers throughout the day and the night, and any suspicious persons must be arrested.
>
> During the night everyone must be particularly careful to prevent fires.
>
> 19 July 1581.[11]

---

9   Kan'ichi Asakawa, *The Documents of Iriki* (New Haven: Yale University Press, 1929), p.321.

10   *HGDK*, p.295.

11   Yasuhiro Nishigaya, *Sengoku no jō 1: Kantō* (Tokyo: Gakken, 1993), pp.17–19.

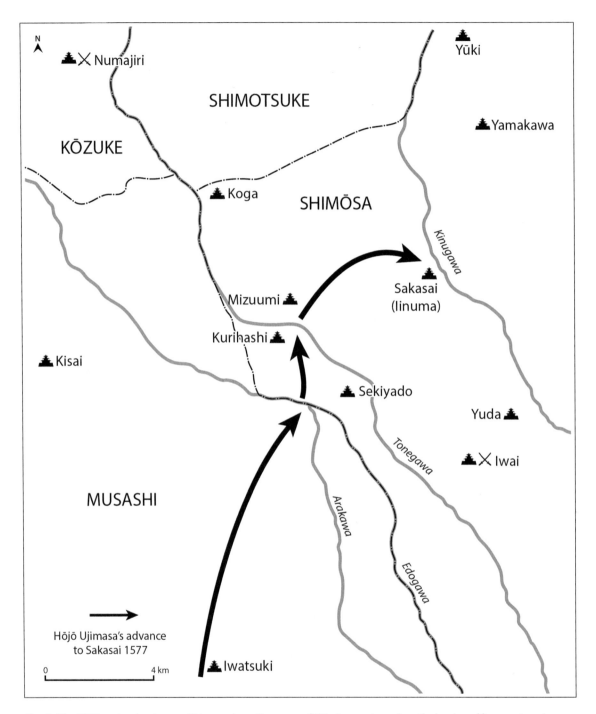

Map 3. The Hōjō's eastern border wars. This map shows the corner of Shimōsa province where the borders of four provinces lay very close together. The land consisted of broad rivers, swamps and rice fields. It was the site of the Hōjō's long-lasting border wars with the Satake and the location of the battles of Iwai, Yuda and Sekiyado. Koga was the traditional seat of the Koga Kubō, the shogun's representative in the east. Sakasai (Iinuma) on the Kinugawa marked the limit of Hōjō influence towards Hitachi apart from a few deeply penetrating raids that were soon abandoned. Hōjō Ujimasa's 1577 advance to Sakasai is shown by an arrow.

Satake Yoshishige (1547–1612) was the daimyo of Hitachi province and engaged the Hōjō in battle on numerous occasions across the swamplands of Shimōsa province. This drawing of him is in Kubota Castle Museum, Akita.

The campaigns against the Satake were characterised by the use of lower class warriors known as kusa, who lay in wait to attack samurai. Their deeds contributed towards the image of the ninja.

It was rare for the raids and skirmishes from these forts to develop into pitched battles. Instead both sides would prudently disengage and then glare at each other until the next affair started, so the actions around the border strongholds required a type of warfare different from the developing trend of organised squads of spearmen and harquebusiers. Many of the operations would be associated with undercover operations by *shinobi*, a tactic that the Hōjō seem to have embraced wholeheartedly, as shown already by the examples at Kawagoe and Kōnodai. The title preferred for *shinobi* in *Hōjō ki* is *kusa*, which literally means grass, because 'they concealed themselves beneath the moss, so they were honoured with the title of *kusa*'.[12]

A classic instance occurred during the autumn of 1571 when Ujimasa confronted Satake Yoshishige in the Iwai district. The Satake had been raiding local villages and burning houses, but when the raids became a nightly occurrence local warriors concealed themselves among the grass and waited for the enemy to pass by:

> Many of the enemy were killed or wounded by them, although not even one of their heads was taken while they themselves took over one hundred enemy heads. These heads were brought to Ujimasa by the *hatamoto* to be inspected and verified. Among the head takers were two farmers of Iwai who had taken the heads of meritorious persons; both of them had pounced on the samurai. Ujimasa commented, 'The taking of samurai heads is an everyday occurrence, but it is unusual for it to be done by peasants. Let the two be summoned.' One of them said, 'Every night we hide in the grass armed with just bamboo spears. We wait for the enemy, thrust at them and take their heads.'[13]

Ujimasa withdrew his armies from the area when it was reported that a Satomi fleet had been sighted off the coast of Izu, but more fighting took place in 1573 not far from Iwai near the strategic castle of Sekiyado, a place that dominated the flatlands and had been fought over for decades. In November of that year the castellan of Sekiyado whom Ujimasa had appointed rebelled and joined the Satake, so the Hōjō marched against him:

> Chiba Tarō Tanemune and the others attacked out of boats from the riverside. They raised their war cry. First in was Chiba Tarō Tanemune who kept advancing even though his armour was pierced through, and finally made it to the castle main gate under a hail of bullets from the defenders. … Tanemune gritted his teeth and kept going forward, but then a harquebus fired from the middle of the fence struck true and he fell. Kikuma Tōshonosuke took his head.[14]

Sekiyado finally surrendered because of a shortage of supplies and ammunition, and from then onwards it remained a key Hōjō base for the border operations against the Satake, for which the fight for the castle of

---

12   *HGDK*, p.314.

13   *HGDK*, p.341.

14   *KK*, pp.258–259.

Fighting between the Hōjō and the Satake is shown in one of the bloodiest depictions of samurai warfare in the whole of *Hōjō Godai ki*. One sword blade cuts a man's unprotected skull clean in two.

Yuda provides a further example.[15] In the autumn of 1574 Hōjō Ujimasa ordered Ise Sadakazu to 'rope off' (i.e. fortify) Yuda village, but Sadakazu's land-clearance operation was unusually ruthless. He selected a very good location for the new castle that allowed provisions and supplies to be taken in easily by boat, but unfortunately the site was already occupied by a much-loved shrine to Tenjin the *kami* of learning. The haughty Sadakazu simply burned the shrine down, an act that caused great resentment among the local people. His followers Kazama Magozaemon and Ishizuka Tōemon were appointed to defend the newly built Yuda with 300 *keisotsu* (low-ranking soldiers) under them. The first name is interesting because he is supposed to be the son of the famous *shinobi* Kazama Kotarō. As a result most modern accounts say that he was in charge of 300 ninja at Yuda, even though the word does not appear in the original reference. Some variations of the story have even relocated him to Sakasai Castle along with his ninja as an added incentive for tourists to visit the restored site![16]

The Yuda area belonged to Tagaya Masatsune, so he sought an opportunity to drive out the enemies who had not only invaded his domain but destroyed an eminent shrine. He first tried bribery to make the garrison surrender, but when that failed Masatsune sent requests for help to Uesugi Kenshin, Satake Yoshishige and Utsunomiya Hirotsuna. In the meantime he paid homage from afar to the *kami* of the destroyed Tenjin shrine, praying for the defeat of his enemies and that good fortune should attend his allies. Masatsune promised that if victory was gained he would restore the shrine precincts to their previous condition, but the Hōjō's garrison at Yuda made the first move by sending 200 men to block the approach of the relieving armies. Masatsune's son observed the manoeuvre and crossed the dried up river bed of the Kinugawa. He cut his way into the enemy while a fellow general took advantage of the Hōjō unit's absence from Yuda:

> Watanabe Suō-no-Kami with the assistance of the locals of Iinuma, attacked and burned the castle of Yuda, killing the garrison beginning with the guard captain. It was completely destroyed. Learning of this, those of the garrison who had gone to block the road at Hanashima tried to retrace their steps, but they could not force their way through the army of the Tagaya father and son. They fell into the deep rice fields and swampy ground and could not get out, so they were trampled underfoot. They fought to the death and perished; their corpses looked like butcher's meat.[17]

Those left alive from the Hōjō garrison, about 100 in all, fought one another as they ran to the boats to escape. After their victory the Tagaya rebuilt the Tenjin Shrine, 'making it into a place pre-eminent in shrine

---

15   *HK*, pp.150–151.

16   One example (in an otherwise exemplary book) is Nishigaya, p.85.

17   *KK*, p.262.

visiting. They dedicated many mirrors and images of Tenjin to the shrine because their prayers had been heard.'[18]

Three years after this reversal Ujimasa succeeded in establishing another forward post a few kilometres to the north by rebuilding the castle called Iinuma that is now known by its original name of Sakasai after being carefully reconstructed. It happened during 1577, the year in which the Hōjō mounted their most intensive operations against the Satake. Sakasai's keeper Hōjō Ujishige was confined indoors due to illness so his son Ujikiyo took command, crossed the Kinugawa and advanced in the general direction of the castles of Yūki and Yamakawa. Hōjō Ujiteru, who was based in Kurihashi Castle, was kept informed and reported to their ally Ashina Moriuji that, 'since the time we left on 1 June and forced our way into the Yūki and Yamakawa districts, there are violent encounters in this area every day. On this occasion we are in for a long haul.'[19]

When Uesugi Kenshin heard of the developments he decided to assault the area in support of the Satake, so on 15 August Hōjō Ujimasa collected a large army from Iwatsuki Castle and marched off to secure Iinuma before Kenshin arrived. According to *Toshima-Miyagi monshō* he led 1,500 men. The army list is highly detailed and provides a snapshot of harquebus deployment for a unit serving outside the protection of a castle's walls. There are 500 mounted samurai, and the troops on foot include 50 harquebusiers serving under two *teppō-bugyō* (commissioners for firearms), which suggests that they are operating in two organised squads. This compares to 40 archers and 600 spearmen, so the proportion of harquebuses is still very low by 1577.[20] We must of course allow for the fact that Ujimasa would not have wished to denude Iwatsuki of its defensive weaponry for his expeditionary force, but the small proportion suggests either a continued reliance on spears and bows in the field or a simple shortage of harquebuses during the late 1570s.

As was so typical of the border wars no clash occurred because Uesugi Kenshin never appeared, so in late August Ujimasa struck camp, but on 16 October the Satake returned to the Iinuma area and engaged the Hōjō in repeated skirmishes. By fighting these battles around Iinuma the Hōjō firmed up their bases for a future advance deep into Hitachi, but a stalemate persisted throughout the winter, and in February 1578 the Hōjō received the welcome news that Uesugi Kenshin had died.

Uesugi Kenshin's passing was a great relief to the Hōjō, but the event promised nothing but tragedy for one of Ujimasa's brothers. As shown by several examples noted earlier, adoption was the way in which a daimyo's son could be used in a manner similar to a daughter's forced marriage. On many occasions adoption worked very well, but one of Ujiyasu's sons suffered in a remarkable fashion when his adoption became mixed up with Takeda and Uesugi politics.

Facing page

Top: Sakasai (Iinuma) Castle had its origins in a minor outpost which Daidōji Suruga-no-Kami captured from Sakasai Tsuneshige, hence the name. In 1577 Ujiyasu ordered Hōjō Ujishige, the son of Tsunanari and the current keeper of Tamanawa, to build a new castle from scratch. Craftsmen came from Fujisawa and Kamakura.

Bottom: One of the reconstructed gate towers of Sakasai.

---

18 *KK*, p.262. The castle was built on swampy ground at a modest height of only 10 metres. The site is now part of Bando Golf Club. The rebuilt shrine has disappeared.

19 Nishigaya, p.88.

20 Udagawa 2013, p.60–65.

Hōjō Saburō (1554–79) was Ujiyasu's seventh son and had first been adopted by his uncle Hōjō Genan, whose own sons had been killed at the battle of Kanbara. At the age of 10 Saburō was sent as a hostage to Takeda Shingen, but when that alliance collapsed he was dispatched back to Odawara. At the time Ujiyasu was actively courting the support of Uesugi Kenshin, so in 1569 Saburō was sent off as a hostage for a second time. Kenshin, who never married, took a liking to the youth and adopted him as his own son under the name of Kagetora.

All went well until Kenshin died suddenly in 1578 without having named his chosen heir. The inheritance was disputed between Kagetora and Kenshin's nephew Kagekatsu, whom Kenshin had also adopted, and matters came to a head at the siege of Otate Castle in 1579. Their armed standoff threatened the entire future of the Uesugi line, so naturally the Takeda and the Hōjō tried their very best to resolve matters to their own advantage. At first the support of his former family of the Hōjō tilted the advantage towards Kagetora, but much hinged on whose cause Takeda Katsuyori would decide to follow. Katsuyori was swayed by a considerable cash bribe of 20,000 gold pieces from Uesugi Kagekatsu, and with Katsuyori's backing Kagekatsu felt secure enough to assault Otate in great force. When Otate fell Kagetora attempted to escape to Odawara and the protection of his birth family, but he was betrayed en route and committed suicide. It was a sad end for a man who had been a political pawn for his entire life.[21]

The Hōjō's campaigns against the Satake would continue for many years, and tensions were still high when the threat from Hideyoshi became apparent during the mid 1580s. In May 1585, for example, Ujimasa attacked Satake's retainer Minagawa Yamashiro-no-Kami after a deep penetration into Shimotsuke province. Some skirmishing took place in an area called Naganuma ('the long swamp'), but both friend and foe found the watery terrain very difficult so neither made a frontal attack, and the only military activity consisted of *shinobi* raids under cover of darkness. Boredom soon set in, at which 'the soldiers set up a riding ground in front of the lines and amused themselves by riding horses, and when the end of summer gave way to autumn fireworks were set off in the enemy camp, so the young warriors of our allies did the same and set off fireworks too'. By then three months had passed, and a messenger came from the Satake side proposing a welcome truce.[22]

The flat borderlands were also ideal for the operation of *monomi no musha* (warrior scouts), who were the Hōjō's highly mobile mounted intelligence gatherers chosen from among the *hatamoto*. To the admiring author of *Hōjō Godai ki* they were 'highly trained horsemen, and exclusively persons of great merit'. In one particular incident during the autumn of 1585 Ujinao selected five scouts who rode off towards the Satake positions. Among them were two horsemen who were familiar with the area called Yamakami San'emonnojō and Haga Hikojirō. They galloped up to a high point from where they could carry out observations and fortunately spotted the enemy's *kusa* lying in wait

Facing page

Top: The main gate of Sakasai is approached across a bridge over the moat.

Bottom: This is the courtyard of Sakasai. In 1580 Hōjō Ujikatsu became Sakasai's keeper. It stayed a Hōjō possession until 1590, but when Hideyoshi invaded the isolated castle was abandoned. The place survived as a river port and is noted in 1611 as providing a harbour for the local tea trade.

---

21   Turnbull, *The Samurai Art of War*, pp.132–135.

22   *HK*, p.176.

The sea battle of Omosu no Ura is shown here as a heroic land encounter fought at sea. We see an interesting vignette of a samurai defending himself against a *naginata* by using a *kusari-gama* (sickle and chain).

for them, who rose up 'like a swarm of bees' to surround the two mounted men and catch them 'like fish in a net'.[23] The *kusa* chased the scouts into a river, and *Hōjō Godai ki* describes how Hikojirō was surrounded but he rode into the river and made his horse swim to safety.[24] The use of scouts and *kusa* were two ways whereby Ujimasa conducted warfare in ways that did not involve the stereotype of named heroes squaring up to each other for single combat. By including these topics *Hōjō Godai ki* provides a good overview of samurai warfare during the Sengoku Period, to set beside the persistence of individual heroics and the development of infantry units.

Takeda Katsuyori and the Fight for Suruga

Far to the west of his domains Ujimasa faced a threat from Shingen's chosen heir Takeda Katsuyori, who had shown his worth on several battlefields. As a fine leader of horsemen he had been instrumental in the victory of Mikata-ga-Hara in 1573, although Katsuyori is of course best known to history for being the loser at the famous battle of Nagashino in 1575. Conventional views have it that the defeat at Nagashino by Oda Nobunaga meant his departure from political and military influence or even the family's total destruction. The reality was very different, particularly for the Hōjō family, whom Katsuyori would fight for several years to come in spite of the fact that they had a very close personal relationship. As part of the earlier alliance with Shingen Ujimasa was married to a sister of Katsuyori and the future daimyo Ujinao was their son. In addition Ujimasa's sister Fujin (1564–82) became Katsuyori's second wife in 1577.

Regardless of such niceties, as master of Suruga as well as Kai, Katsuyori sought to outdo his father and drive the Hōjō out of Izu province, which had been the Hōjō's heartlands since the days of Sōun. In the autumn of 1579 Katsuyori set out from Suruga against Izu. The remaining months of 1579 and on into 1580 witnessed a wide range of military activity at locations beneath Mount Fuji including noble single combat, a fierce naval battle and some lively undercover raids.

The incident involving single combat is recorded for the battle of Ukishima ga Hara when the skilled archer Suzuki Kikyōnosuke killed Aoki Kakuzō of the Takeda. *Hōjō Godai ki* describes it in the style so cherished in samurai tradition of a mounted archery feat, even though it was probably conducted out of the overall run of the battle and may even have hindered the achievement of a victory. Suzuki Kikyōnosuke first spotted a victim who appeared to be worthy of his attentions and issued a challenge. Aoki Kakuzō responded appropriately, and a lively mounted archery contest began with little reference to what was going on around them. Each warrior was accompanied only by his closest retainers, and Kikyōnosuke's sent an arrow through Kakuzō's shoulder. He

---

23   *HGDK*, p.396.

24   *HGDK*, pp.396–397; Turnbull, *The Samurai Art of War*, pp.160–163.

Ujiyasu's daughter Fujin (1564–82) became the second wife of Takeda Katsuyori (1546–82). His last battle was at Tenmokuzan in 1582, where Fujin committed suicide along with her husband.

toppled from his horse. Messengers were sent back to both commanders telling them of the samurai heroism that the armies had just witnessed.[25]

The sea battle took place in the third lunar month of 1580 between the Takeda and the Hōjō navies in Suruga Bay, just off the coast from Omosu no Ura. The text describes solid wooden warships from which *ōdeppō* were discharged with great effect together with normal-sized harquebuses fired down from the towers on the ships. Loopholes were set into the ships' superstructures for protected firing. Victims of the Hōjō attack were submerged up to their waists as their ships filled with water, while bullets and arrows 'fell like rain'. It was no place for challenges to single combat.[26]

The irregular warfare on land was carried out using *shinobi* here called *rappa*.[27] They were led by the notorious *shinobi* Kazama Kotarō, who was mentioned above in connection with Kawagoe. He is described as 'a giant who cannot be concealed among his 200 men. His eyes appear to be upside down, he has black whiskers, and his mouth is particularly wide at the sides. Four of his fangs stick out. His head resembles Fukurokuju [one of the seven gods of good luck] and his nose sticks up.'[28] The first character of the word *rappa* means disorder and the second means a wave, and it was indeed as a wave of disorder that they hit Katsuyori's encampment. 'Every night or so they crossed the wide Kisegawa and entered secretly into Katsuyori's camp. They captured people alive and cut through the ropes tethering the horses, which they rode bareback, plundering and raiding.'[29] Takeda Katsuyori tried to hit back against Kotarō and his *rappa* by using *kusa*, who tried to capture Kazama as he made his way back with the booty. The ambush was not a success, because the 10 *kusa* were discovered and killed before they tried to attack. Their defeat made Kotarō even bolder, and for the rest of the Izu campaign he kept the Takeda troops in a state of nervous tension whenever night fell.[30]

Katsuyori's reversals in Izu and Suruga proved to be a portent of disaster both for him and for his family's future. *Hōjō Godai ki* describes something very strange about Katsuyori's retreat from Izu in the face of a threat of intervention by Tokugawa Ieyasu, because a broken-hearted Katsuyori destroyed his own equipment including the Takeda flags so that they would not fall into the hands of his enemies. The picture of the scene shows Katsuyori sitting forlornly on his camp stool while an elaborate tiger-skin quiver, a suit of armour and bundles of pole-arms are thrown onto the bonfire. As Katsuyori is wearing only his armour robe it could well be his own expensive suit of armour that is being destroyed; the Hōjō would have made much of such a trophy.[31] The armies of Oda Nobunaga and Tokugawa Ieyasu then pushed him deeper and deeper into the mountains. His last battle was at Tenmokuzan in 1582, by which time

25 *HGDK*, p.398; Turnbull, *The Samurai Art of War*, p.138.

26 *HGDK*, pp.352–354.

27 *HGDK*, p.381; Turnbull, *The Samurai Art of War*, pp.140–143.

28 *HGDK*, p.399.

29 *HGDK*, p.399.

30 *HGDK*, p.400.

31 Turnbull, *The Samurai Art of War*, p.146.

A slave raid is launched into Hōjōterritory by the hated Satomi. The sordid practice of kidnapping and abducting people of one's own kind to use as forced labourers was referred to as 'slave harvesting'.

he had lost most of his hereditary retainers and generals. Totally overwhelmed, Katsuyori committed *seppuku*. His wife Hōjō Fujin committed suicide along with her husband and the Takeda line came to an end.

The Satomi Sea Raids

Throughout this time the Hōjō also faced armed encounters from the Satomi that involved raids across the sea as in the attack on Kamakura in 1526, but by this time a system of beacons had been established to give warning. The beacons burned wolf dung, which produced very dense black smoke. The alert was then further conveyed through the nearby villages using war drums and conch shell trumpets, at which the inhabitants took up arms.[32] *Hōjō Godai ki* explains why these warnings were so necessary, because they could often be accompanied by the abduction of men and women as slaves. Bands of irregulars joined the regular foot soldiers in a daimyo's army to carry out these acts of indiscriminate pillaging and enslaving, and it is more than likely that most areas of Japan saw some violence of this sort. The Satomi raiders rowed across in small boats during the night to raid the coastal settlements, seizing women and children and putting to sea while it was still dark. So regular were the raids that the local inhabitants came to a private understanding with the Satomi to pay 'protection money' to get back the hostages.[33] Along with the massacre at Fukane this was the sordid reality of Sengoku conflict to set alongside the glorious heroics of legend and the application of up-to-date military technology.

---

32   *HK*, pp.343–345; Turnbull, *The Samurai Art of War*, p.122.

33   *HGDK*, p.350; Turnbull, *The Samurai Art of War*, p.168.

9

Hōjō Ujinao and the Threat from Hideyoshi

Throughout the 1570s the Hōjō had watched safely from the Kantō while Oda Nobunaga won victory after victory and laid the foundations for the reunification programme that Hideyoshi would complete, but the situation changed drastically following the death of Takeda Katsuyori in 1582. Nobunaga was the one who had brought about the destruction of the Takeda clan, so he took over their former provinces of Kai, Shinano, Suruga and parts of Kōzuke. That brought him perilously close to the Hōjō domain for the first time in their shared history, and it was the latter province in particular that caused concern to the Hōjō. At first suggestions were made for a marriage alliance with Nobunaga in return for the cession of territory, but that idea came to nothing because Oda Nobunaga had his own ideas about how the former Takeda territories should be administered. In spite of protestations from the Hōjō, he gave the western half of Kōzuke and two districts of Shinano to Takigawa Kazumasu (1525–86).[1]

Hōjō Godai ki devotes several paragraphs of its account of the war against Kazumasu to a denunciation of his evil deeds in the past. As daimyo of a domain in Ise province, Kazumasu had been instrumental in Nobunaga's thorough conquest of neighbouring Iga province in 1581, where he was alleged to have massacred three- and four-year-old children.[2] In the 1659 *Hōjō Godai ki* Kazumasu is pictured celebrating his new appointment in the Kantō by performing a chant from a Noh play in front of his feasting retainers,[3] but his joy was to be cut short by news of the death of his master Oda Nobunaga that same year. Another of Nobunaga's generals had turned traitor and attacked the temple where Nobunaga was resting. Overwhelmed by the raid, their great leader had committed suicide.

The death of Nobunaga threw the capital into confusion, and Hōjō Ujimasa guessed that Kazumasu was now dangerously isolated from any support.

---

1   *HGDK*, pp.355–359.

2   *HK*, p.169.

3   Turnbull, *The Samurai Art of War*, p.154.

Kazumasu controlled two important castles in Kōzuke: his capital of Minowa and the equally strong fortress of Matsuida. Hōjō Ujikuni led the attack on Minowa from Hachigata, 'raising his war cry and thrusting forward his cross-bladed spear'.[4] The ferocity of the Hōjō operations succeeded in driving Kazumasu out of the Kantō forever, and in 1583 Hōjō Ujinao followed up his expulsion of the intruder by defeating another Kōzuke landowner called Kitajō Takahiro at Maebashi. This placed the Hōjō in control of almost all of Kōzuke except the territory owned by the Sanada in the north of the province. In accordance with the Hōjō satellite system, Minowa became a support castle for Hachigata.

Hōjō Ujinao was the last of the five Hōjō daimyo, and was spared death when the castle fell.

The death of Nobunaga also meant trouble in the west of the Hōjō domains, because his passing had brought their western borders closer to those of Tokugawa Ieyasu, and tensions between them grew in a similar manner to the Takigawa episode. Kawajiri Hidetaka (1527–82) had been Nobunaga's appointee to Kai province after the death of Katsuyori, but when the locals revolted and put him to death Ieyasu took advantage of the situation and marched into Kai to claim it for himself. This alarmed Hōjō Ujimasa, who sent two separate armies into Kai and confronted the Tokugawa with daily exchanges of gunfire at a place called Wakamiko.[5] Major bloodshed was avoided thanks to the intervention of Ujimasa's brother Ujinori (1545–1600), who knew Ieyasu very well, having once been a child hostage with him in the custody of the Imagawa. Successful negotiations followed which resulted in the ceding of Kai and Shinano to Ieyasu while the Hōjō were recognised as rulers of most of Kōzuke. The Hōjō/Tokugawa peace agreement was confirmed the following year when Ieyasu married his daughter to Hōjō Ujinao. Not unexpectedly, the Hōjō coveted the whole of Kōzuke and fought Sanada Masayuki (1547–1611) on three occasions during the 1580s, but they invariably failed to subdue him.

The Origins of the Odawara Campaign

The expulsion of Takigawa Kazumasu from Kōzuke and the successful negotiations with Ieyasu would prove to be the last significant triumphs that the Hōjō would ever enjoy, because within days of Nobunaga's death he had been replaced by someone far more threatening. Toyotomi Hideyoshi's seizure of power began from the moment of his defeat of Nobunaga's usurper at the battle of Yamazaki. Hideyoshi's fellow generals were hopelessly

---

4   *HK*, p.172.

5   Shin'ichi Saitō, *Sengoku jidai no shūen: 'Hōjō no yume' to Hideyoshi no tenka tōitsu* (Tokyo: Yoshikawa Kōbukan, 2019), pp.35–37; *HK*, p.174.

Above: Minowa Castle became a Hōjō possession following the expulsion of Takigawa Kazumasu from the Kantō. (Public domain)

Right: Tokugawa Ieyasu (1543–1616) was the father-in-law of Hōjō Ujinao, but that did not excuse him from leading the Tōkaidō Division during Hideyoshi's Odawara Campaign. Ieyasu took over the Kantō when the Hōjō were defeated.

divided, so he picked them off one by one in a series of rapid campaigns. The subjugation of Shikoku was carried out in 1585, followed by the conquest of the great southern island of Kyushu in 1587. The Hōjō of Odawara were Hideyoshi's next target. His invasion of the Kantō would be the greatest test of the Hōjō's military abilities that was ever mounted, and it was the one which they failed.

The Odawara campaign of 1590 took place during the reign of Ujinao, who became the fifth daimyo when his father retired a few months before Hideyoshi's onslaught. The Hōjō were anything but complacent (overconfident may be a more accurate expression) but in contrast to Hideyoshi's strategic vision and detailed planning, the behaviour of the Hōjō leaders at the time presents a picture of division and poor decision-making. Indecision, in fact, lay at the heart of Hōjō governance, because Ujimasa was no autocrat and discussed serious matters of state with the senior retainers on his *hyōjō* (council). The body had been established in 1552 to adjudicate on fairly minor matters, but by the mid 1580s it was considering much weightier issues such as the appropriate response to make to Hideyoshi's threats. Consensus always proved difficult, to the extent that the expression 'an Odawara council' is used proverbially in Japan nowadays to indicate a conference or debate that is long-winded and ends up going nowhere.[6]

Ujimasa's Odawara Council met three times between 1585 and 1590 to discuss the Hideyoshi situation. The first meeting during June 1585 considered the straightforward question of whether the Hōjō should submit to Hideyoshi's demand to become his vassals. This was of course two years before the Shimazu of Satsuma would surrender to Hideyoshi and survive (albeit after being defeated in a huge military campaign) so the Hōjō had no precedent to follow. Ujimasa accordingly refused to visit Hideyoshi or to make any sign of obeisance. Hōjō Ujinori would eventually be sent to Kyoto as an envoy three years later, so in 1585 the Hōjō may have been playing for time while they made their own military preparations.

At the time the Hōjō were still involved in the border wars described above, but there are enough references to Ujimasa and Ujinao preparing their domain against Hideyoshi from the mid 1580s onwards to confirm that they took his threats seriously, even if they were unable to decide exactly what to do about them. One of the Hōjō's great strengths was their satellite castle system, and much important information about the Hōjō's preparations at this stage in the campaign may be found in documents relating to Hōjō Ujikuni's Hachigata. Unlike most of the other provincial castle keepers, Ujikuni was not ordered to Odawara when Hideyoshi invaded but would stay in Hachigata, where defensive preparations are recorded as early as 1586. Because of Hachigata's role as a provincial support castle Ujikuni also had to send messengers to all the castellans of its subordinate castles in Kōzuke and northern Musashi ordering them to review their defences.[7] The local

---

6   Birt, 1983, p.56.

7   *SSKS*, p.657.

Delegates from Hōjō Ujimasa bring diplomatic gifts to Oda Nobunaga. The Hōjō samurai kneel respectfully in front of the great general, their swords placed safely at their sides while grooms tend their horses. The gifts include two hawks.

strategic situation was complex, because Sanada Masayuki still posed an immediate threat to the Hōjō regardless of any future moves by Hideyoshi.

Documents of the time also reveal the fine details of how Hachigata was maintained. In 1586 Ujikuni ordered his retainer Chichibu Magojirō to repair a stretch of Hachigata's walls, plus one tower and three gates in that section. The rules were strict. If the man was a part-time soldier who was away on campaign, his wife and servants had to make the repairs. Typhoon damage, which was likely to be very serious, required instant attention, and on those occasions they had to make the repairs on the castle immediately even if their own homes had been destroyed. The domain's needs always came first.[8] Ensuring sufficient food supplies was also a matter of the greatest importance, so in the autumn of 1587 Ujikuni ordered the villagers of Kitadani in Kōzuke to collect and store all the grain gathered from the fields around Minowa.[9] At about the same time Ujikuni reviewed the operational readiness of his part-time companies. The Arakawa-*shū*, for example, had to present themselves for inspection on the first day of the fourth lunar month of that same year along with all their weapons, which had to be in first class condition.[10]

Other records indicate a marked increase in the manufacture and distribution of harquebuses throughout the Hōjō domain from about 1587 onwards. An excellent example of the response in Kōzuke is provided by an order concerning Ujikuni's third-level support castle of Gongenyama, which was subordinate to Minowa.[11] Gongenyama was one of the Hōjō's outermost frontier posts and covered any hostile approaches from the nearby castles of Numata and Nagurumi, both of which were owned by Sanada Masayuki.

Inomata Kuninori (?–1590) had been placed in charge of Minowa following the ousting of Takigawa Kazumasu. His first order concerning Gongenyama is dated 31 May 1588 and informs his follower Yoshida Shinza'emon Masashige that Masashige's existing 100 *kan* stipend is being replaced by one of 150 *kan*, from which Masashige has to use 100 *kan* to furnish a 20-man harquebus squad at the castle.[12] The remaining 50 *kan* was to fund Masashige's promotion to commander of Gongenyama along with a fitting personal entourage of six spearmen, one archer, one harquebusier and one flag bearer.[13] Sometime during June 1588 Masashige entered Gongenyama to take charge of what had now become a 255-man garrison of 27 horsemen, five other samurai, 202 ashigaru and Masashige's newly created harquebus squad of 20 men.[14]

Five months after Masashige's arrival two retainers called Esaka Matabei and Matsumoto Jihei compiled a detailed inventory of Gongenyama's arsenal

8   *SSKS*, p.646.

9   *SSKS*, p.682.

10 *SSKS*, p.674.

11 Not to be confused with the castle of the same name in Musashi province which was contested between the Hōjō and the Uesugi in 1510.

12 *SSKS*, pp.703–704; Udagawa 2013, p.68.

13 *SSKS*, p.710.

14 Nobuaki Tamaru (ed.), *Senryaku, Senjutsu, Heiki Jiten* (Tokyo: Gakken, 1994), pp.117–118.

滝川左近一益

In spite of all the protestations by the Hōjō, Nobunaga gave the western half of Kōzuke Province and two districts of Shinano to Takigawa Kazumasu (1525–86). Hōjō Ujimasa then launched an attack on Kazumasu which succeeded in driving him out of the Kantō forever.

116

to send to Inomata Kuninori. The weapons list they produced is almost unique in its detail and is one of the most valuable pieces of evidence for the number and types of firearms that could be deployed in a small castle of the time. The report is divided into three sections: the castle's existing arsenal, the weapons sent over from Hachigata and Nakayama castles to strengthen Gongenyama because of its frontline position, and equipment supplied by Yoshida Masashige himself. Already in stock within Gongenyama were the following items (present author's comments in parentheses):

1 *ōdeppō* (large-calibre harquebus)

50 *teppō*

69 *ōdeppō* shot (although these particular ones are noted as consisting of two normal *teppō* shot wrapped in paper to make one large bullet)

1,200 prepared gunpowder charges

1,350 'black metal' bullets (i.e. bullets for normal-calibre *teppō*)

The materials brought in from the other castles were as follows:

900 similar bullets; brought over from Hachigata Castle and received by Esaka Matabei

68 large bullets (presumably for the *ōdeppō*), ditto

14 *hō* ('shots' of gunpowder), ditto

9 *kin* – 9.4 kg of prepared gunpowder charges, ditto

1,500 arrows, among which are 500, ditto

10 bows supplied from Nakayama Castle

Yoshida Masashige supplied the following arms and equipment from his own resources on his appointment to Gongenyama Castle:

15 *teppō*

1,500 prepared gunpowder charges

1 *hako* (box) of saltpetre

3,200 bullets

Above: Hachigata's proximity to disputed Kōzuke province made it a key satellite fortress. Here we see the reconstructed moat and fence.

Below: Hachigata had originally been owned by the Fujita. Hōjō Ujikuni was adopted into the family, and in 1564 he was assigned to Hachigata where he introduced stone into important parts of its defences. This model in the modern Hachigata Castle museum shows the castle's dramatic location above the river that acted as its moat on one side.

20 spears, wooden-shafted (for foot soldiers)

10 spears, bamboo-shafted (for foot soldiers)

2 *mochi-yari* (spears for mounted samurai)

2 *mochi-hata* flags (for samurai)

12 flags for foot soldiers

100 arrows

3 bows

1 quiver

20 'cut bullets'

2 *yagen* (mortars)

100 sheets of iron

10 [bags of] food supplies[15]

The inclusion of saltpetre and two mortars for grinding suggests that further supplies of gunpowder would be manufactured within the castle itself; the necessary sulphur and charcoal would presumably be obtained readily from local sources. The sheets of iron were probably intended for making bullets, as will be discussed below. 'Cut bullets' had been damaged or badly forged and needing a final rounding off. According to Udagawa they would have been left with pronounced corners that would be smoothed by being beaten and rolled in oiled paper. The figures for 65 harquebuses compare very favourably with the castle's total stock of 30 long-shafted spears for the foot soldiers, showing that by the late 1580s their deployment was clearly regarded as more important than spears.[16] Yet firearms were not everything, and additional orders were issued in 1588 that warned about an infiltration by 500 *suppa* (i.e. *shinobi*) from Shinano.[17]

Other documents from about this time illustrate how the Hōjō's very efficient intra-domain system of packhorse post stations aided the transport of raw materials to the busy gunfounders. During April 1586 there are records

---

15 *SSKS*, p.714.

16 Tamaru, pp.117–118 and Udagawa 2013, pp.67–70.

17 Iwata, pp.11–12. This document does not include a year in the accompanying date, and has been placed in the Saitama documents collection under the year 1582. Iwata however believes that this is unlikely because Shinano was then secure. He suggests instead that it refers to the ongoing threat from Sanada Masayuki and the preparations against Hideyoshi (accessed 4 July 2022).

of the transportation from Ōiso to Odawara of a mysterious consignment of 'soil' for use in the production of *nakazutsu* (medium-sized harquebuses). Udagawa believes that the word 'soil' indicates a particular form of sand for making fireproof moulds for gunfounding. On 28 October 1587 an order was issued for 35 packhorse loads of unspecified materials for gunfounding to be sent from Ōiso to gunsmiths in Odawara, and in the following year on 8 February 1588 a further 24 packhorse loads of materials for casting bullets set out on the five day journey along the same route.[18] These were to be delivered to an individual identified only as 'Sudō', who must be the gunsmith Sudō Sōza'emon Moriyoshi, the son of the late Sudō Sōza'emon Morinaga. His father had been a master craftsman who had served as a silversmith (among other accomplishments) under Hōjō Ujitsuna and then made the transition to gunfounding.[19] So great was the demand for metal for casting into guns and bullets that in 1588 the temple bell of Moro Daimyōjin in Musashi province was requisitioned for melting down by Hōjō Ujiteru, the keeper of the newly established Hachiōji Castle. Archaeological excavations at the Hachiōji site have revealed fragments of a temple bell that had probably been broken up in this way to supply metal for casting bullets.[20]

Efforts to manufacture more harquebuses within the domain were stepped up when the threat from Hideyoshi became imminent. Early in 1590 a certain Yamada Jirōza'emon, who appears to be acting as a supervisor of craftsmen, issued an order to 14 named gunsmiths in Sagami province to make 20 *ōzutsu*, the large-calibre versions of harquebuses otherwise called *ōdeppō*. Four of the gunsmiths had to make two each; three more made one apiece while the others produced four and five respectively by combining their efforts. These heavy weapons were most suitable for castle defence and would probably have been intended for Odawara.[21]

It is also important to note that firearms were not supplied to the Hōjō army solely by men of samurai rank as part of their feudal obligations. Many bows, spears and harquebuses were stored away ready for action in the smallest of the villages within the Hōjō domain by the part-time *jizamurai* (warrior-farmers) on whom Ujimasa depended to make up the bulk of his armies. No concerns were ever raised about any possible danger of rebellion that might arise from the villagers' ownership of weapons. The Hōjō domain was a different environment from the not-too-distant future, when Hideyoshi's notorious Sword Hunt forced anyone who was not in the emerging samurai class to be completely disarmed. The only punishment the Hōjō's subjects had to fear would be that meted out to an able-bodied man who failed to present himself for the selection process, a fate that could include decapitation. The situation is revealed in one such call to arms issued by Ujimasa in the summer of 1587 to the villagers in the district of Sawara in Sagami province. The order, which bears the official tiger seal of the Hōjō daimyo, is not a muster list for

---

18   Udagawa 2013, p.66.

19   Birt 1983, pp.42, 235.

20   Udagawa 2013, p.67.

21   Udagawa 2013, p.66.

a landowning warrior; instead it is an obligation placed upon all the male inhabitants between the ages of 15 and 70, out of whom four have to be chosen for service in the army. The villagers have to bring along whatever weapons they possess, including harquebuses. The entire Hōjō domain would have to face up to Hideyoshi.[22]

Toyotomi Hideyoshi (1537–98) unified Japan, for which the defeat of the Hōjō was a major step forward. This statue of him is in the grounds of Osaka Castle.

Hideyoshi's Preparations

Meanwhile Hideyoshi was making his own preparations for war, but at this stage his moves were more political than military, and Hideyoshi was temporarily distracted when a series of rebellions broke out in newly pacified Kyushu. Sassa Narimasa, to whom Hideyoshi had given half of Higo province, had handled his new responsibilities so badly that he managed to provoke a

---

22 *SSKS*, p.677. The original document may be viewed at *Hōjō-shi tora impanjō*, Yokosuka City website <https://www.city.yokosuka.kanagawa.jp/8120/bunkazai/shi30.html> (accessed 22 September 2021).

revolt which needed considerable resources to quell.[23] The Higo Rebellion was followed by a further uprising on the Amakusa Islands which took until 1590 to bring under control, and Hondo Castle on Amakusa only surrendered to Hideyoshi's generals the day after he declared war on the Hōjō.[24]

Of far more relevance to the Kantō area was an incident in Kōzuke that provided Hideyoshi with a useful excuse for chastising the presumptuous Hōjō. Nagurumi was a Sanada-owned castle located 10 km from Numata on the opposite bank of the Tonegawa, and it enters the story when Hōjō Ujinori journeyed to Kyoto to visit Hideyoshi. Ujinori was in a conciliatory mood, and informed Hideyoshi that if the Numata district was handed over to the Hōjō then Ujimasa and Ujinao would visit Hideyoshi in his Kyoto palace. Hideyoshi took this as a gesture of submission so, keen to receive the Hōjō lords and accept their homage, he agreed. Sanada Masayuki was ordered to hand over to the Hōjō two-thirds of his territory in northern Kōzuke including Numata. He would retain the remaining third that included the district and castle of Nagurumi. It appeared to be a very favourable deal for the Hōjō, but the agreement was not all it seemed to be. Hideyoshi was a ruler who thought far ahead, and it is more than likely that he had already made the decision that when his showdown with the Hōjō was finished he would give all their territories to someone else, as would indeed happen.

In accordance with his promise Hideyoshi sent a messenger to Sanada Masayuki on 31 August 1589 ordering him to hand over Numata to the Hōjō. Masayuki complied meekly and Hōjō Ujimasa gave Ujikuni responsibility for the place. Ujikuni in turn delegated the castle down the satellite fortress hierarchy to Inomata Kuninori, the keeper of Minowa. Kuninori had thus been placed in a position of some influence, but in November he took the extraordinary step of annexing Sanada's district of Nagurumi and its castle in direct defiance of Hideyoshi's ruling. The author of *Hōjō ki*, who clearly blames Kuninori for the misfortunes that followed, calls him a 'rustic warrior lacking in both wisdom and discernment' for disobeying Hideyoshi and setting the invasion in motion.[25]

Suitably enraged by the Nagurumi Incident, Toyotomi Hideyoshi officially declared war on the Hōjō on 31 December 1589, and on 5 January 1590 he held a council of war with the three key daimyo who would play a major role in the forthcoming operation. The first was Tokugawa Ieyasu, whose domain lay adjacent to the Hōjō's. Having avoided service in the invasions of Shikoku and Kyushu Ieyasu could hardly refuse to be involved in the Odawara campaign, even though his daughter was married to Hōjō Ujinao. Ieyasu's army would approach Odawara along the Tōkaidō, the Pacific coast road, together with Hideyoshi's nephew Toyotomi Hidetsugu

---

23 Stephen Turnbull, *Tanaka 1587: Japan's Greatest Unknown Samurai Battle* (Warwick: Helion, 2019).

24 Stephen Turnbull, 'The ghosts of Amakusa: localised opposition to centralised control in Higo province, 1589–90', in *Japan Forum* 25 2, pp.191–211.

25 *HK*, p.181.

(1568–95), Oda Nobukatsu (1558–1630), Asano Nagamasa (1546–1611) and several others.

The other key daimyo were located in the Hokurikudō region to the north of Kyoto on the coast of the Sea of Japan. The first was Uesugi Kagekatsu, the heir to Kenshin and the destroyer of Kagetora. The second was Maeda Toshiie (1538–99), one of Hideyoshi's ablest generals and a man who does not appear to have had any prior dealings with Odawara. Together with Toshiie's son Toshinaga (1562–1614) and Sanada Masayuki, who was still smarting from the Nagurumi Incident, they made up the Hokurikudō Division who would approach Odawara from the north-west. Elsewhere Nagatsuka Masaie (1562–1600) was given the responsibility of overseeing all supply issues during the campaign, while Kuki Yoshitaka (1542–1600), Katō Yoshiaki (1563–1631), Wakizaka Yasuharu (1554–1626) and Chōsokabe Motochika (1539–99) were named as admirals of Hideyoshi's fleet who would blockade Odawara from the sea.

The Hōjō leaders called a meeting of their council early in 1590. They now faced a situation of imminent invasion, and its members split into two factions. The first group favoured withstanding a siege; the second advocated marching out to stop Hideyoshi's army somewhere in the Hakone Mountains. Matsuda Norihide favoured the former course of action. Others preferred the latter option, and among them was Hōjō Ujikuni of Hachigata. A letter from him to Chichibu Magojirō illustrates the dilemma in which someone like Ujikuni had been placed by the emergency. Ujikuni has no alternative but to ask his follower for even more men and resources for the defence of their small corner of the domain.[26]

Once again no decision was made one way or another within the Odawara Council, which meant that the siege option was made by default, because no army marched out of Odawara before the first hostile troops appeared at its gates and decided the issue for them. Instead a reverse movement of forces happened, because the commanders of almost all the outlying Hōjō fortresses were recalled for service at Odawara along with hundreds of their followers. With a few notable exceptions the satellite castle system that had served the Hōjō so well for decades was abandoned in terms of what had once been its prime purpose: the defence of the realm. The departure of soldiers from the provincial castles for the walls of Odawara also had the unintended effect of leaving unprotected their wives and children, who were now vulnerable to being taken as hostages by Hideyoshi's advancing army. It is by no means clear why the decision was made to concentrate so many military resources in Odawara. It is even possible that no real decision was made at all and that Hideyoshi's advance directed every aspect of Hōjō policy from that time onwards.

---

26 *SSKS*, p.706.

10

The Fall of the House of Hōjō

The first units of Hideyoshi's army of invasion set off early in March 1590 for what history would call the Odawara Campaign. Popular myth portrays the operation as a bloodless pushover because the Hōjō eventually surrendered after a long and largely peaceful blockade of Odawara Castle. The sources, however, including the *gunkimono* accounts, call this image into question. The siege of Odawara may have developed into a tedious standoff, but the battles to reduce the weakened satellite castles were ruthless, violent and bloody. One by one the places whose history was recounted in previous pages either surrendered, were captured or were abandoned. The latter fate befell all the minor forts at the edge of their domains; so Sakasai and Gongenyama played no role in the defence of the domain. Perhaps surprisingly, *Hōjō Godai ki* covers the attacks on the provincial castles very briefly. *Hōjō ki* provides much more information, and its stark inclusion of details such as the crucifixion of prisoners pulls no punches.

The Advance Along the Tōkaidō

The Tōkaidō Division left for Odawara on 6 March 1590. Tokugawa Ieyasu issued a number of strict regulations concerning keeping order in the ranks and the avoidance of disruption to the civilian population. There was to be no looting. This may seem a very noble sentiment, but they were his own territories through which his army was marching! Weapons also had to be carried according to set rules and horses had to be controlled. Sadler provides a vivid illustration of how discipline was maintained when a splendidly dressed samurai who was not keeping order on the march was summarily relieved of his head.[1]

Hideyoshi left Kyoto on 5 April with the main body of the army. He issued orders three days later that his navy, who had already entered Shimizu Bay on 1 April, was to reconnoitre the coastline of Izu province. Hideyoshi reached Ukishima ga hara on 1 May, and on arrival at Mishima on 2 May he ordered

---

1   A. L. Sadler, *The Maker of Modern Japan* (London: Allen and Unwin, 1937), p.162.

the capture of Nirayama and Yamanaka. The former was an intensely symbolic prize because it had once been Hōjō Sōun's chosen fortress. It would also become the last castle but one to surrender when it capitulated on 25 July, having held out defiantly behind Hideyoshi's front line throughout the entire campaign. Guns were stationed at its loopholes and at the tops of towers from where fire could be directed on to the attackers. The wording of the *Kanhasshū kosenroku* account implies that a rotational system of loading and firing was used for both large- and small-calibre weapons that 'penetrated both shield and armour'. One of their victims was a follower of Gamō Ujisato who was hit in the side by a volley of bullets so that 'his blood flowed out like a waterfall'.[2]

Nirayama may have threatened Hideyoshi's communications from the south, but the other key castle in Izu lay right on the Tōkaidō itself. This was Yamanaka, and its strategic location on the western slopes of the Hakone range high above Mishima made it effectively the Hōjō's first line of defence against the invaders. Yamanaka, which has recently been excavated and landscaped, consisted of a long line of outer defence works along a gradually rising ridge that culminated in a group of connected baileys (*maru*). The defensive areas were divided from each other by wet moats and ditches, and some of the latter still show their characteristic divided checkerboard pattern designed to hinder an enemy's progress.

Yamanaka Castle had been founded by Hōjō Ujiyasu and was defended in 1590 by Hōjō Ujikatsu (1559–1611), a grandson of Hōjō Tsunanari. It was attacked on 3 May by troops under Toyotomi Hidetsugu and Tokugawa Ieyasu, and fell after only a few hours of intense fighting. Separate units attacked different areas of the castle hill at the same time, and *Kanhasshū kosenroku* notes that a prominent general called Hitotsuyanagi Naosue was shot dead by a bullet fired from Yamanaka's walls.[3]

Greater detail about the Yamanaka operation is supplied by the unique eyewitness account of Watanabe Kanbei (1562–1640). He was a retainer of Nakamura Kazuuji (?–1600) and wrote about Yamanaka in a personal testimony called *Watanabe Suian oboegaki*.[4] Kanbei was no armchair samurai. The Yamanaka attack is something he experienced in person, and even if he probably exaggerated his own role in the achievement of victory, Kanbei's route through the defences as recorded in his blow by blow account can be traced to this day among the castle ruins.

Watanabe Kanbei's attack may be reconstructed as follows. While other units of the Tōkaidō Division were concentrating on the Nishi no maru (western bailey), Kanbei began his personal quest for glory at the very tip of the southern outer defence works called the Taizaki demaru (*demaru* means a detached bailey). He first came under fire when his men were digging trenches from which to launch their assault. Kanbei suggested to Nakamura Kazuuji that the defences were weak. Their route then took them up to the San no maru

---

2   *KK*, pp.441–442.

3   *KK*, p.436.

4   Tōshirō Ōta (ed.), Hanawa Hokinoichi (1746–1821), *Watanabe Suian oboegaki*, in *Zoku Gunsho Ruijū*, vol. 20 (Tokyo: Zoku Gunsho Ruijū Kanseikai, 1923), pp.490–523.

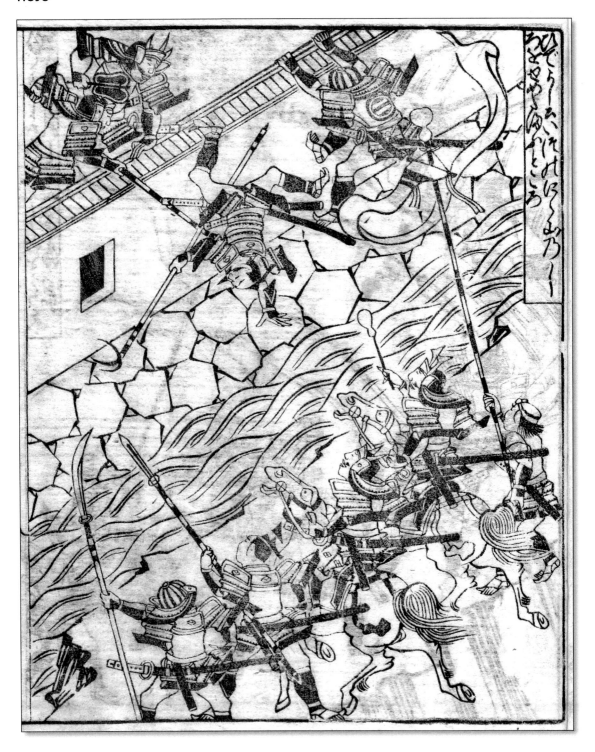

Toyotomi Hideyoshi's army attacks Nirayama Castle, which would hold out to the very end.

(third bailey), which had an offset gateway and was protected by an abattis of felled trees. Harquebus fire was coming from two directions so Kanbei took cover. More samurai joined him, but four of them were shot dead on the way. Kanbei estimated the range of the garrison's harquebuses to be about 30 *ken* (54.6 metres), within which he and his comrades could not operate in safety. The continuing gunfire resulted in between 50 and 60 other men being struck by bullets, leaving some dead.

After a while the firing ceased, and when the smoke dispersed Kanbei took the opportunity to move round the outside of the San no maru and lead an assault over the wall. This tactic was successful, and it soon became apparent to the attackers that the Hōjō troops were withdrawing across a bridge into the Ni no maru (second bailey). Kanbei pursued them and observed a large number of 'armoured warriors' in the Ni no maru, an expression which probably indicates that the San no maru had been defended largely by ashigaru. He was determined to acquire a prestigious enemy head, which would mean taking the fighting into the Hon maru (inner bailey), but at that stage Kanbei did not know in which direction the Hon maru lay within Yamanaka's complex layout. He climbed a cedar tree to make observations, and noticed that one of the adjacent baileys contained a large building and was defended by about 200 men. It was also the direction from which most of the gunfire was coming. Concluding that this must be the heart of the fortress, Kanbei made his way in by some means and at some point (the bridge connecting it to the outer defence works had been demolished), relying on his prominent *sashimono* banner to indicate his position to his followers. Kanbei claims that his arrival – spear in hand – forced the defenders to retreat to the tower at the rear that acted as the castle's keep. Fighting bravely, his unit approached the tower, and the castle surrendered when other attacking units entered the Hon maru from the captured western bailey. Yamanaka's commander Hōjō Ujikatsu was dissuaded from surrender by his followers, and instead escaped through the northern gate of Yamanaka and retreated to Tamanawa.[5]

Archaeological excavations at the site of Yamanaka Castle have confirmed the extensive deployment of harquebuses by both sides during the battle, and the finds also provide important information about the types of bullets used there. Out of 188 bullets excavated from Yamanaka, 25 were cast from lead, 16 were of iron, while 147 were of a lead/copper alloy. Lead bullets were the most common type used during the Sengoku Period because their low melting point allowed easy casting and the prospect of recycling spent rounds. The alloy bullets, which were 74 percent copper and 18 percent lead plus some nickel, had a higher melting point and therefore suggest the presence on site of specialist bullet casters. These alloy designs would have had greater penetrating power against armour.[6]

5   Ōta, pp.494–498.

6   Tamaru, pp.88–89.

Above: A section of the model of Yamanaka Castle in Kanagawa Prefectural History Museum, showing the ridge along which Watanabe Kanbei launched his attack.

Facing page, top: An excavated section of Yamanaka's moat, showing the chequerboard design that hindered an enemy's progress by laying them open to gunfire.

Facing page, bottom: The reconstructed bridge between the San no maru (third bailey) and Ni no maru (second bailey) of Yamanaka Castle.

On 6 May, three days after the fall of Yamanaka, the first units of the invading army from the Tōkaidō Division took up their positions around Odawara. Hideyoshi was now well on his way and arrived at Yumoto on 9 May where he visited the Sōunji, the memorial temple of the founder of the dynasty he had come to destroy. Meanwhile other Tōkaidō units bypassed Odawara and pressed on to Tamanawa and Edo, both of which surrendered on 29 May. Their armies then marched against Kawagoe and Iwatsuki. Usui Castle in Shimōsa, where the 'Matsuda Red Devil' had once bettered Uesugi Kenshin, also surrendered to the Tokugawa force at about this time. That left one major fortress objective in this area of the Kantō. The place was Oshi Castle, which depended for its defences on the marshes and stretches of water that surrounded it. Showing that he had learned much in the service of Hideyoshi, who had reduced other castles by inundation, Ishida Mitsunari (1559–1600) converted the defensive waterways into an offensive weapon and flooded the place. This took time, however, and Oshi did not surrender until after Odawara had fallen, succumbing on 15 August as the last of the Hōjō fortresses to capitulate to Hideyoshi.

The Advance from the North

Uesugi Kagekatsu rode out of Kasugayama Castle on 15 March and Toshiie began his journey 10 days later. Their Hokurikudō Division entered the Kantō when they crossed the border into Kōzuke province on 22 April and began to capture all the castles in Kōzuke except Tatebayashi which lay isolated at its extreme eastern point. Numata was first to fall, followed by Maebashi, Matsuida and Minowa. The Hokurikudō Division then marched straight into northern Musashi, where the keeper of Matsuida was forced by Maeda Toshiie to act as the invading force's guide.

Their first target in Musashi was mighty Hachigata. Troops under Uesugi Kagekatsu and Maeda Toshiie spread 35,000 troops around the castle on 14 June, and after a month-long siege Hōjō Ujikuni (who is believed to have had command of only 3,000 men) surrendered on 15 July.[7] Ujikuni was taken prisoner by Maeda Toshiie and would be conveyed to Toshiie's Kanazawa Castle after the siege of Odawara had ended along with his adopted son Ujisada and his trusty retainer Machida Yasutada. Ujikuni died at Kanazawa in 1597 as one of the few survivors from the Hōjō inner circle, at which Yasutada committed *junshi*, the ritual act of suicide to follow his master in death.

There are almost no details in the chronicles about the 1590 operation against Hachigata, but local tradition tells us that during the siege Ujikuni used eight dogs as messengers between the main castle and its outposts with the written communications tied to their collars in bamboo tubes, just as had been done at Matsuyama. When the castle fell the four surviving dogs wandered hungrily around the area and the local people took pity on them.

---

7   Nishigaya, p.69.

A shrine was erected, and a memorial service was held annually when the names of the dogs were recalled along with an invocation of Amida Buddha:

Ōgō, Ōrai: Namu Amida,
Yūzuma, Fukuzama: Namu Amida,
Tsutsuki, Tsumabuki: Namu Amida,
Chūya, Manpuku: Namu Amida.

The four dogs called Yūzuma, Fukuzama, Tsutsuki and Tsumabuki died during the battle. It is said that in 1781 the memorial service was neglected, at which white feathery down from the persimmon tree beside the shrine floated into every nearby house as if it were white dog hair. Since that time the ritual has been performed every year.[8]

Matsuyama Castle was the next to fall at the end of June, but this time there was no brave exchange of poetry between opponents. Instead Matsuyama surrendered to Maeda Toshiie as peacefully as Hachigata had done, although the wives and children of its leaders were seized as hostages.[9] By contrast, the mountain fortress of Hachiōji put up a fierce resistance against the Hokurikudō Division. Hachiōji was a relatively new foundation in western Musashi that dated only from 1587 after nearby Takiyama had been abandoned because of its comparatively weak position. Hachiōji's commander Hōjō Ujiteru was not present when Hideyoshi attacked it but was in Odawara, where it was believed that he was most needed. The optimistic Ujiteru reckoned that Hachiōji's topography would enable it to withstand an attack, and the castle was indeed well situated, with its main approach being along a narrow valley through which rushed a river. The attackers suffered rocks being dropped on to them from cleverly located *ishiyumi* (stone-dropping holes).[10]

Fifty thousand men attacked Hachiōji's garrison of only 1,300. It is usually hyperbole to say that the river ran red with the blood of the slain, but in the case of Hachiōji it may literally have been true when the corpses fell into the narrow mountain stream. Ghost stories abound in connection with Hachiōji, with tales of the sounds of hoofbeats and fighting being heard long after the battle had finished. The women of the castle jumped to their deaths from the towers rather than be captured by Hideyoshi's forces and, according to legend, on the anniversary of the battle (24 July) the waters of the river turn red once again.[11] Archaeological excavations carried out at Hachiōji Castle add to the impression of desperate resistance given by the legends. The bullets exchanged between the Hōjō and Toyotomi forces included very few lead bullets and about twice as many alloy bullets compared to iron ones,[12] but Udagawa also

---

8   Aoyagi Kenji Photo blog, <http://asiaphotonet.cocolog-nifty.com/blog/2019/05/post-7ec5ba. html> (accessed 9 September 2022).

9   *HK*, p.196.

10   *HK*, p.197.

11   More legends about Hachiōji's fall may be found at <https://www.tazunearuki.info/hachioji-castle/legend.html> (accessed 20 September 2022).

12   Tamaru 1994, p.89.

Right: The Saitama dog shrine, erected in memory of the canine warriors of Hachigata.

Below: This reconstructed bridge at Hachiōji spans the mountain stream which flowed red from the blood spilt during the terrible siege of 1590.

includes photographs of clay bullets found at Hachiōji, which may indicate a degree of desperation on the part of the beleaguered garrison.[13]

Hachiōji therefore ended with a bloodbath, but the most terrible story to come out of Hideyoshi's campaign against the satellite castles concerns the siege of Iwatsuki by Asano Nagamasa. Iwatsuki was commanded by Ujimasa's brother Ujifusa, who had been adopted into the Ōta family. He sent a letter to Odawara requesting help on 25 July, pleading that even 'fathers, mothers, women and children' were actively involved in the castle's defence. Iwatsuki was not going to surrender quietly.[14] According to *Hōjō ki*, the attack was launched across the wet moat at a spot which Hideyoshi's scouts had found to be reasonably shallow. The troops were met by volleys of gunfire. When the castle fell the wives and children of the defeated garrison were seized and taken to Odawara, where for some reason that is not made clear they were crucified in front of the walls in full sight of the defenders.[15]

The Siege of Odawara Castle

The area of ocean around Odawara was secured by a sea battle on 26 May off Shimoda while Hideyoshi was in the process of constructing the most complex siege lines in Japanese history. He described them in a letter to his wife, where he reveals that he is already thinking beyond Odawara towards a campaign in Ōshū (northeastern Japan):

> We have surrounded Odawara with two or three rings and have constructed a pair of moats and walls, and we do not intend to let a single enemy out. People from the eight provinces of the Kantō are entrenching themselves there, and so if we succeed in starving Odawara into surrender, the way to Ōshū is so wide open that I cannot but be satisfied.[16]

So great was the throng outside the walls of Odawara that the barricades became a town in their own right where the besiegers sang, played games, enjoyed theatrical performances and were permitted to have their wives with them. Hideyoshi explained this policy in the letter to his wife, whom he asked to make arrangements for his favourite concubine Lady Yodo to come to Odawara also.[17] With all the comforts of home within the siege lines, the besiegers loudly proclaimed their wealth of wine, women and song to the miserable defenders whenever they had the chance to move within earshot. As noted above, these confident scenes designed to encourage Odawara's surrender were of course accompanied by the sight of the crucified bodies of

---

13 Udagawa 2007, p.33.

14 Umezawa 2012, p.142.

15 *HK*, pp.203–204.

16 Adriana Boscaro, *101 Letters of Hideyoshi* (Tokyo: Monumenta Nipponica Publications,1975), p.37.

17 Boscaro, p.38.

The reconstructed wall of Odawara Castle. Odawara was well supplied with guns that would have been fired through loopholes similar to those reproduced here.

the families of the defenders of Iwatsuki. On the defenders' side (at Ujimasa's own suggestion) a daily market was set up in the grounds of the Matsubara Daimyōjin to encourage morale among Odawara's inhabitants. As far as Hideyoshi was concerned, all he had to do was wait. The garrison of Odawara just had to keep calm and carry on.

As the days went by the confident Hideyoshi firmed up his plans for the resettlement of the Kantō after the Hōjō's inevitable surrender, and *Kanhasshū kosenroku* relates a colourful incident in this vein. Hideyoshi led Tokugawa Ieyasu to a vantage point overlooking the castle and took his hand. Hideyoshi then explained that when the Hōjō surrendered he would give Ieyasu lordship over the eight provinces of the Kantō. 'Good,' replied Ieyasu. 'Let's piss on the bargain.' So the two of them turned in the direction of the enemy, stood side by side and struck a deal in the agreed manner. 'From this time onwards,' says *Kanhasshū kosenroku*, 'Hideyoshi and Ieyasu have been known as 'the pair who pissed on the Kantō'.[18]

It cannot have been easy for Ieyasu to have agreed to relinquish his ancestral home of Mikawa province along with the lands in Tōtōmi, Suruga, Shinano and Kai that he had acquired by supreme effort. Nor is the gift likely have been a spontaneous gesture on the part of Hideyoshi in the way that the chronicler implies. Confident of victory, and already looking beyond Odawara to the one-third of Japan that made up the country's north-east, Hideyoshi – the supreme strategist – had long decided how he was going to resettle the conquered provinces. Tokugawa Ieyasu would become Hideyoshi's Kantō Kubō, although in reality the entirety of the eight provinces would never be Hideyoshi's to give, because among his key supporters in the area were the Satomi in Awa together with Utsunomiya and Nasu in Shimotsuke. The loyal

---

18   *KK*, p.450.

Sano, too, owned lands in Kōzuke, while Satake was the daimyo of Hitachi. Hideyoshi had no intention of depriving them of their lands – for now.

Odawara, of course, still had to surrender and was a formidable fortress. Miura Jōshin provides some figures for its dimensions in 1590. From east to west the castle stretched for 50 *chō* (5,450 m) and from north to south (where it touched the sea) for 17 *chō* (1,850 m) within an outer defensive perimeter of five *ri* (almost 20 km). Towers soared high above its stone walls.[19] As noted above, three harquebuses were stationed at every loophole in Odawara's walls with one *ōdeppō* in between them.[20] Elsewhere Miura Jōshin confirms that among its garrison 600 men of the Hōjō *hatamoto* stood ready 'fully armoured and with a bow, a harquebus or a spear in every hand'.[21] He also notes *ōdeppō* in particular being fired from the loopholes,[22] while the clamour of the war cries, the harquebuses and the bows (in the stock phrase) 'echoed between heaven and earth'.[23]

The only description in *Hōjō Godai ki* of intensive combat during the siege of Odawara is an account of fierce hand-to-hand fighting in what was otherwise a process of patiently wearing down the defenders. The attack in question was led against one of the outer baileys of Odawara by Ii Naomasa (1561–1602) of the Tokugawa force. Miners from Kai tunnelled under and brought down a section of the walls. Protected by what Jōshin calls 'iron shields', which were probably ordinary large wooden shields reinforced with iron plates against Odawara's harquebus balls, Naomasa's army threw bundles of grass and reeds into the moat and attacked the breach under heavy gunfire. There were many casualties among the attackers, including some who were shot dead when they became trapped in the brushwood entanglements that acted as the barbed wire of their day. The Ii troops broke in and set fire to buildings, and there was much hand-to-hand fighting. Following this episode, Jōshin tells us, the siege settled down to sporadic exchanges of arrows and bullets.[24]

Finally, thanks to Miura Jōshin (who may well have been present on the occasion), *Hōjō Godai ki* contains a unique example of a poem inspired by gunfire. It was composed during a lively firearms exchange on the night of 19 June, the sight of which prompted Hōjō Ujimasa to ascend one of Odawara's towers and express his feelings in verse. His poem translates as follows:

Have the stars fallen from the skies?
Are there fireflies beside the moat?
No, it is just the flashes of gunfire![25]

---

19 *HGDK*, pp.363–364.

20 *HGDK*, p.295.

21 *HGDK*, p.363.

22 *HGDK*, p.364.

23 *HGDK*, p.368.

24 *HGDK*, p.371.

25 *HGDK*, p.296.

Overleaf: In this detail from *Ehon Taikō-ki* the besiegers of Odawara mock the garrison inside the walls by demonstrating their wealth of food and drink.

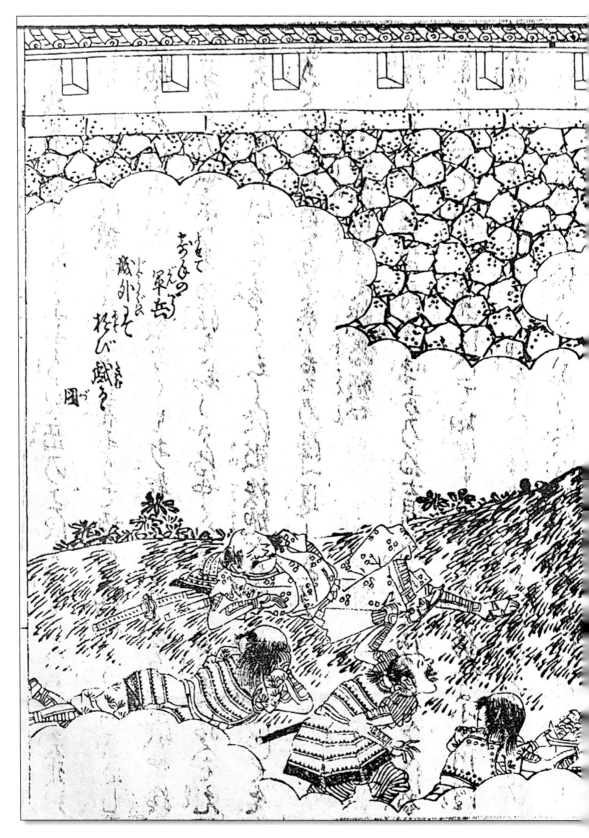

Samurai inside the keep of Odawara pass the time sharpening and polishing their swords or playing *suguroku* (backgammon). Two others are enjoying a game of *go*. Their suits of armour are ready to be donned at a moment's notice. *Sashimono* also stand ready to be slotted into their holders, while quivers, harquebuses and bows are leaning against the rearward wall.

Ii Naomasa (1561–1602) of the Tokugawa force leads an attack across the moat of Odawara Castle. Bundles of twigs and stones are tipped into the ditch to make a solid causeway.

Not all of Ujimasa's commanders acted with similarly poetic stoicism, and much criticism has been levelled against Matsuda Owari-no-Kami Norihide. He was the Hōjō's most senior retainer and was so trusted that he was allowed to use the daimyo's seal on official documents. The siege of 1590 found him inside Odawara Castle, from where he engaged in negotiations with Hideyoshi. Norihide was wise enough to appreciate the inevitable outcome, but critics interpreted his *realpolitik* as treason. According to *Hōjō Godai ki* Norihide turned traitor and offered to open the gate he was guarding in return for the provinces of Izu and Sagami, but his son heard of the plan and denounced his father to Ujinao. A separate unit of Hōjō samurai with no connection to Norihide were immediately deployed to the gate in question. When Hideyoshi's men arrived the gate was opened as expected, but not to let them through. Instead a fierce sally by the waiting defenders was launched that drove Hideyoshi's stunned and disappointed assault party into the moat.[26]

The Revenge of the Rivals

One little known aspect of Hideyoshi's Odawara campaign concerns the behaviour of the Hōjō's long-standing enemies in the neighbouring provinces. These lords were the 'people from the Kantō' mentioned above in Hideyoshi's letter to his wife. They had fought the Hōjō for decades and happily grabbed the opportunity provided by Hideyoshi's invasion to pay back a few old scores. Shimotsuke provides the example of Utsunomiya Kunitsuna (1568–1608), who had lost almost all his territory to the Hōjō by 1590. When Hideyoshi invaded the Kantō Kunitsuna joined in with the siege of Oshi and was richly rewarded. Also to be found in Shimotsuke was Nasu Sukeharu (1557–1610) of Karasuyama Castle, but he failed to read the signs of the times and delayed pledging support for Hideyoshi until after Odawara had fallen. To Hideyoshi this was tantamount to supporting the Hōjō, and only special pleading allowed the Nasu name to continue in the person of his son. The settlement came at the price of the loss of Karasuyama in return for a much-reduced domain.

Over in Hitachi the Hōjō's old enemy Satake Yoshishige had handed control of their territory to his son Yoshinobu in 1589. They were threatened from the north by Date Masamune (1537–1636) and from the south by Hōjō Ujinao, so Hideyoshi was seen as something of a saviour. The Satake therefore announced their submission to the invader and helped his campaign directly when Yoshinobu joined Ishida Mitsunari at the siege of Oshi. When Hideyoshi concluded his campaign the Satake firmed up control over their part of Hitachi with his blessing.

---

26 HGDK, p.376; Turnbull, *The Samurai Art of War*, p.192.

Satomi Yoshiyasu (1573–1603) on the Bōsō peninsula was not so fortunate. When Hideyoshi invaded the Kantō he hastened to seize any remaining Hōjō possessions in Kazusa and raided the Miura peninsula in imitation of his great-grandfather's notorious attack on Kamakura.[27] That must have helped the invasion effort, but Hideyoshi appeared less than pleased. Yoshiyasu was reprimanded for having acted without Hideyoshi's permission and with no coordination with his plans. As a punishment Hideyoshi reduced Yoshiyasu's holdings to Awa province. That sounds extremely harsh, but it was probably all part of Hideyoshi's grand strategy. He had already decided that when the Hōjō were defeated he would give Kazusa to Ieyasu as part of his fief of the Kantō.

The Sano family and their castle of Karasawayama also re-enter the story during Hideyoshi's invasion. It will be recalled that when Sano Munetsuna had died unexpectedly Hōjō Ujimasa sent his brother Ujitada to be adopted as the Sano heir. That decision aroused huge resentment on the part of Sano Fusatsuna (1558–1601), the late Munetsuna's younger brother, who left the province along with several of his retainers. The 1590 campaign provided the opportunity for him to hit back. The exiled Fusatsuna was living in Kyoto, so Hideyoshi promised him the restoration of the Sano fief. In return Fusatsuna supplied Hideyoshi with information about the Kantō including detailed sketch maps, and when Hideyoshi set out for Odawara Fusatsuna acted as a willing local guide. Fusatsuna then took part in the siege of Oshi, which certainly seems to have been a popular choice for deployment among the anti-Hōjō faction in the Kantō! The roll call of the besiegers includes the names mentioned above together with representative from the families of Yūki, Tagaya and Mizunoya.[28]

The current keeper of Karasawayama on the Hōjō's behalf was Sano (Hōjō) Ujitada, but he was summoned to Odawara by Ujimasa, leaving its defence in the hands of former Sano retainers. When Hideyoshi's army attacked only one of the defenders stayed loyal: a man known in the literature as the Daikan ('Magistrate') Echigo-no-Kami. Defence was impossible, so he committed *seppuku* when the castle fell. After the surrender of Odawara Hideyoshi kept his promise to Sano Fusatsuna, who finally became the lord of Karasawayama. He died in 1601.[29]

The Fall of Odawara

A third meeting of the Hōjō Council was held during July when the siege was at its height, by which time the situation had greatly deteriorated. The issue placed before its members was now a stark choice between surrendering to Hideyoshi and fighting to the bitter end. Again no agreement was reached, and one further month of privation would have to be endured before the inevitable decision was forced upon everyone.

---

27 Manabe 2018, p.23.

28 *KK*, p.495.

29 *HK*, pp.200–202.

松田左馬反
さまたさむ
をそむ
こ国つ

In this detail from *Ehon Taikō-ki* Matsuda Norihide's son pleads with his father not to betray the Hōjō to Hideyoshi.

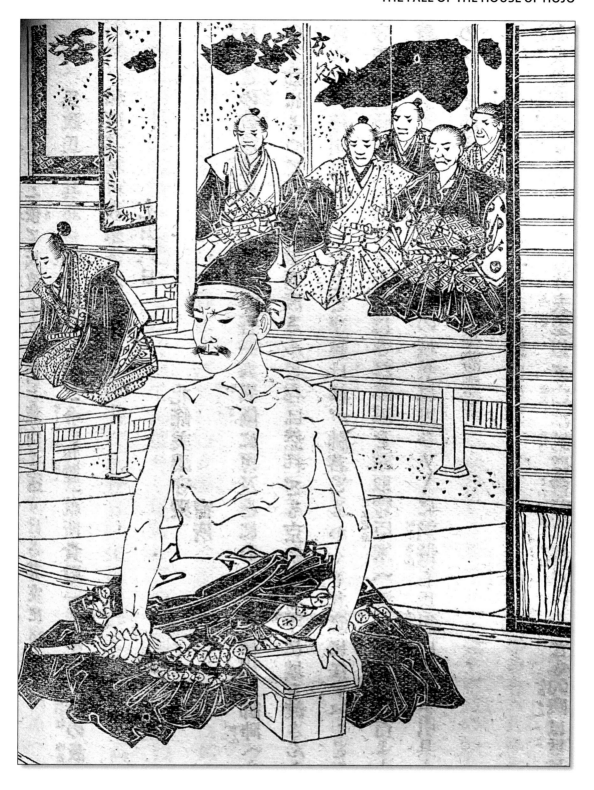

The suicide of Hōjō Ujimasa was a requirement insisted upon by Hideyoshi and was committed in some style when Odawara surrendered.

Odawara Castle finally capitulated to Hideyoshi after detailed but largely one-way negotiations. Ujinao had offered to surrender if they could keep the three provinces of Musashi, Sagami, and Izu, but Hideyoshi was having none of it, and all discussion ceased on 7 July. The final terms were harsh: as part of the surrender agreement Ujimasa and his brother Ujiteru had to commit suicide, and they kept their side of the bargain in some style. Ujimasa thrust his knife deeply into his abdomen while his other brother Ujinori cut off his head. Ujinori had been instrumental throughout the negotiations with Hideyoshi, and with that act he provided the crowning mercy for the defeated dynasty.[30] As Miura Jōshin puts it (without too much exaggeration) the Hōjō had ruled the Kantō for 100 years and lost it in 100 days.[31]

Hōjō Ujinao was spared death, probably thanks to the pleas of his father-in-law Tokugawa Ieyasu. As he left Odawara for exile he quoted a poem attributed to Prince Munetaka who was deposed as shogun in 1266. The prince, who was a puppet shogun under the first family to call themselves Hōjō, had compared his own fate to that of a tiger who had been transformed into a mouse. The irony would not have been wasted on Ujinao, whose dynasty had now completed a century-long transition from rat to mouse via a tiger.[32]

Ujinao was exiled to the holy mountain of Kōyasan, where he died from smallpox in 1591 as the last of the Odawara Hōjō, but the name would continue in the person of his chosen heir Hōjō Ujimori, the son of Ujinori. Ujimori would however have no further connection either with Odawara or anywhere else in the Kantō. Instead his allotted territory was Sayama in Kawachi province near modern Osaka, and future generations who bore the name of Hōjō would rule Sayama under the shogun Tokugawa Ieyasu and his descendants. The traditional use of 'Uji' in their given names was maintained until the last Sayama daimyo Hōjō Ujiyuki (1845–1919) surrendered his fief to the Meiji government in 1869.

The Resettlement of the Kantō

The Hōjō had gone, but Hideyoshi had already taken steps to ensure that they had left no empty space into which the northern daimyo could rush. Having the benefit of hindsight, it is tempting to see the fall of the Hōjō as the final move in Hideyoshi's war of reunification, after which the surrender of the vast provinces to the north of Odawara became merely a footnote to his inevitable triumph, but that was not how Hideyoshi viewed the situation. His mood was sombre, because in the unconquered lands beyond the Kantō there still remained a handful of strong daimyo who had fought each other for decades as if they were living on another planet. Yet as the months went by the image of Toyotomi Hideyoshi as the ruthless conqueror of the Hōjō,

---

30 Turnbull, *The Samurai Art of War*, p.194.

31 *HGDK*, pp.378–379.

32 *HGDK*, p.379.

The graves of the five generations of the Hōjō daimyo lie at the temple of Sōunji in Yumoto.

(not to mention his edicts concerning land ownership, weapon possession and social status), began to concentrate several minds.

In reality their collapse had already begun with the submission of their strongest member: Date Masamune, who arrived as a supplicant in Hideyoshi's camp while the siege of Odawara was still in progress. His pledge of allegiance and subsequent reinvestment in his own territories spared him from destruction. Masamune's surrender was the precedent that Hideyoshi needed, and more capitulations were to come before he was forced to move north. For example, Nambu Nobunao (1546–99) was located in Sannohe Castle in Mutsu province at the northern tip of Honshu. Following Masamune's lead he had an audience with Hideyoshi and pledged his allegiance. Most of the other northern lords followed suit, but Kunohe Masazane of Kunohe Castle in Mutsu refused to accept the new regime and rose in revolt. Hideyoshi dispatched an army under Toyotomi Hidetsugu. It was the furthest north that his troops were ever to march, and the uprising was quickly crushed. There were to be some similar incidents in the far north of Japan for a decade to come, but these were essentially diehard protests against the new regime of resettlement and taxes that Hideyoshi imposed through his local representatives. That Japan was now reunified was not open to question.

There were also no doubts when it came to the future control of the Kantō. When the campaign began Toyotomi Hideyoshi had promised the eight provinces to Tokugawa Ieyasu, and the promise was kept when the Hōjō surrendered. The Tokugawa therefore became the new lords of the Kantō from 1590 onwards, but when it came to choosing his headquarters Ieyasu feared that Odawara's geographical vulnerability might outweigh its prosperity, and decided instead to set up his capital in Edo. He moved in soon after the siege ended.

Toyotomi Hideyoshi died in 1598. His heir was a young child, and the daimyo split into two camps over his succession. The matter was settled at the Battle of Sekigahara in 1600, where the victor was Tokugawa Ieyasu. Unlike both Hideyoshi and Nobunaga, Ieyasu was of a lineage that allowed him to revive the post of shogun, which he did in 1603. With that act, and his firm decision to make Edo the capital of his new Tokugawa Bakufu, the centre of gravity of Japanese politics shifted back sharply to the east, and there it has stayed to this day. In 1868 Edo became Tokyo, the seat of the new Meiji emperor and the capital of modern Japan, right in the heart of the ancient Kantō plain. It was the greatest compliment that anyone could have paid to the strategic vision of the Kantō's most celebrated rulers: the five generations of the Hōjō who had been its supreme samurai warlords.

Epilogue: The Hōjō and Japan's Military Revolution

In 1487 Hōjō Sōun led an attack on a fortified wooden mansion using bows and arrows. In 1590 his great-great-grandson Hōjō Ujinao defended a stone castle using firearms. Between those dates the Japanese art of war had changed out of all recognition and the Hōjō had changed with it, embracing the military revolution as wholeheartedly as any of their contemporaries, although we search in vain in the *gunkimono* to see much evidence for developments in military technology. The omission may simply be that authors like Miura Jōshin did not regard such matters as suitable material for their heroic narratives. Throughout *Hōjō Godai ki,* for example, the inclusion of harquebus fire as a background to brave combat with bows and swords tends to be expressed using stock phrases, whereby noble samurai are met by a 'hail of bullets' which 'echo between heaven and earth', but carry on regardless. References to individual deaths from gunfire normally involve 'a lucky shot' or 'a random bullet' from an unnamed inferior, and Jōshin tends to refer to the weapons under other circumstances only when he lapses into nostalgia for the good old days when gunpowder was a mystery.[1] He never quite reaches the level of scorn that Cervantes put into the mouth of Don Quixote, who lamented 'an invention which allows a base and cowardly hand to take the life of a brave knight … discharged perhaps by a man who fled in terror from the flash the accursed machine made in firing',[2] but Jōshin clearly cherished a time when guns were few in number and arrows hit their mark.[3] Elsewhere he muses that 87 years had passed between the demonstration of the first firearm in the Hōjō domain and his own time when 'they are owned by all and sundry'.[4] It is only in his accounts of the latter years of the Hōjō hegemony and the threat from Hideyoshi that Jōshin gives any impression that harquebuses are now being employed on a large scale in organised firearms squads.

---

1   *HGDK*, p.380.

2   Miguel de Cervantes Saavedra, J. M. Cohen (transl.), *Don Quixote* (Harmondsworth: Penguin, 1950), p.344.

3   *HGDK*, p.380.

4   *HGDK*, pp.296, 295.

As the pages above have shown, the military revolution embraced by the Hōjō definitely included the deployment of firearms in organised units, the widespread use of intelligence gathering and the establishment of a castle network with good communications under trusted commanders. These trends paralleled similar movements in Europe that saw the development of large infantry-based armies, dedicated firearms squads and castles built in the *trace italienne* style. Yet in spite of all these achievements the Hōjō failed the greatest military challenge of their age. The experience of a century spent behind the Hakone Mountains and the state-of-the-art defences of Odawara had made them complacent and not a little haughty in the face of Hideyoshi's awesome military capability, and among those failings was the abandonment of the satellite castle system. In years gone by the fortresses had provided a means of settling and ruling conquered territories. In 1590 the network may well have provided a coordinated defence in depth, but when faced with overwhelming odds attacking from different directions the castles were denuded of support in favour of Odawara and fell one by one.

But were the Hōjō also old-fashioned warriors? Their use of firearms would suggest not: Odawara's angled stone walls allowed good fields of fire and were packed with gunpowder weapons by 1590. Like most of their contemporaries the Hōjō still deployed skilled horsemen and some of them may have preferred bows to spears, but their noble skills (developed partly by the useful pursuit of chasing dogs) would have been fatally undermined if previous generations had neglected to develop infantry tactics for those in the army who did not wield spears from horseback. Far from being guilty of neglecting firearms or failing to organise their infantry, the Hōjō provide an excellent and highly detailed example of the processes involved in their deployment.

A combination of arms under good generalship had been one of the key factors that had allowed the Hōjō to conquer the Kantō within the space of one century. A fortunate combination of strong primogeniture and numerous progeny – factors absent from many of their rivals – had also helped. As with all the other daimyo, the secret of success lay not in the mere possession of new weapons and large armies but in how they were used, and that required financial resources, discipline and the coordination of effort both on and off the battlefield. The third daimyo Hōjō Ujiyasu may have entertained some conservative views, but he was not to blame for his grandson's defeat by an overwhelming force under the man who alone possessed the vast resources needed to achieve the reunification of Japan.

Bibliography

Primary Sources

Primary sources used only sparingly are referenced under the secondary work in which they are quoted. Those used repeatedly in this book are as follows:

HGDK: *Hōjō Godai ki*, in Tatsuo Hagiwara (ed.), *Hōjō shiryō shu* (*Sengoku Shiryō Sōsho*, vol. 1) (Tokyo: Jinbutsu Ōraisha, 1966), pp.215–439

HK: *Hōjō ki*, in Tatsuo Hagiwara (ed.), *Hōjō shiryō shu* (*Sengoku Shiryō Sōsho*, vol. 1) (Tokyo: Jinbutsu Ōraisha, 1966), pp.10–214

KK: Kazunori Nakamaru (ed.), *Kanhasshū kosenroku* (*Sengoku Shiryō Sōsho*, vol. 15) (Tokyo: Jinbutsu Ōraisha, 1967)

SSKS: *Shinpen Saitama-ken shi*, Saitama Prefecture, *Shinpen Saitama-ken shi. Shiryō-hen 6: Chūsei 2: Komonjo 2 Sengoku* (Saitama: Saitama-ken, 1980)

Secondary Sources

Andrade, Tonio, 'The Arquebus Volley Technique in China, *c.* 1560: Evidence from the Writings of Qi Jiguang', *Journal of Chinese Military History* 4, 2015. pp.115–141

Araki, Eishi, *Higo kunishū ikki* (Kumamoto: Shuppan Bunka Kaikan, 2012)

Asakawa, Kan'ichi, *The Documents of Iriki* (New Haven: Yale University Press, 1929)

Birt, Michael Patrick, *Warring States: A Study of the Go-Hōjō Daimyo and Domain, 1491–1590*, PhD Thesis, Princeton University, 1983

Birt, Michael Patrick, 'Samurai in Passage: The Transformation of the Sixteenth-Century Kanto', *Journal of Japanese Studies* 11, no. 2, 1985, pp.369–99

Boscaro, Adriana, *101 Letters of Hideyoshi* (Tokyo: Monumenta Nipponica Publications, 1975)

Bōsō Shōso Kankō Kai, 'Bōsō Satomi Gunki', in *Bōsō Shōso* vol. 2: *Gunki*, Chiba: Bōsō Shōso Kankō Kai, 1950, pp.269–426.

Cervantes Saavedra, Miguel de; Cohen, J. M. (transl.), *Don Quixote* (Harmondsworth: Penguin, 1950)

Conlan, Thomas, *Not So Secret Secrets: Three Uesugi documents (komonjo) of 1559* (Princeton: Princeton University, <http://komonjo.princeton.edu/uesugi/> (accessed 26 May 2021)

Dixon, J. M., 'Kōnodai and its spots of interest', *Transactions of the Asiatic Society of Japan* 10, 1881, pp.39–47

Hirano, Akio, *Mikawa Matsudaira Ichizoku* (Tokyo: Shinjinbutsu Oraisha, 2002)

Hitachi-Ōta City, *Hitachi-Ōta shi shi* (Hitachi-Ōta City:Hitachi-Ōta Publications, 1979)

Ienaga, Junji, *Hōjō Sōun no sujō wo sageru* (Tokyo: Shinjinbutsu Ōraisha, 2005)

Inamura, Yoshitaka (ed.), *Ōu Eikei gunki* vols 1 and 2 (*Sengoku Shiryō Sōsho* vols 3 and 4) (Tokyo: Jinbutsu Ōraisha, 1996)

Iwata, Akihiro, 'Sengoku shinobi wo ou', 2021 <https://ranzan-shiseki.spec.ed.jp/wysiwyg/file/download/1/1223> (accessed 13 September 2022)

Izawa, Shōji, *Odawara no katchū.* (Odawara: Meicho Shuppan, 1980)

Kang, Hyeokhweon, 'Big Heads and Buddhist Demons: The Korean Musketry Revolution and the Northern Expeditions of 1654 and 1658', *Journal of Chinese Military History* 2, 2013, pp.127–189

Kitamura, Akihisa, et al., 'Late Holocene uplift of the Izu Islands on the northern Zenisu Ridge off Central Japan', *Progress in Earth and Planetary Science* 4, 30, 2017, pp.1–17

Kuroda, Motoki, *Sengoku Hōjō Godai* (Tokyo: Ebisu Kōshō Shuppan, 2013)

Kuroda, Motoki, *Sengoku Hōjō ke ichizoku jiten* (Tokyo: Ebisu Kōshō Shuppan, 2018)

Kuroda, Motoki, *Zusetsu Sengoku Hōjō-shi to kassen* (Tokyo: Ebisu Kōshō Shuppan, 2018)

Manabe, Junya,*Miura Dōsun: Ise Sōsui ni tachihadakatta saidai no raiburu* (Tokyo: Ebisu Kōshō Shuppan, 2017)

Manabe, Junya, *Sengoku Edo wan no kaizoku: Hōjō suigun vs Satomi suigun* (Tokyo: Ebisu Kōshō Shuppan, 2018)

Matsuda, Kiichi and Momota Kawasaki (transl.), *Kanyaku Furoisu Nihon shi* vol. 10 (Tokyo: Chūōkōron-Shinsha, 2000)

Murdoch, Sir James, *A History of Japan* vol. I, 2nd impression (London: Kegan Paul, Trench and Trubner, 1925)

Nakamura, Kōya, et al. (eds), *Kōyō Gunkan* vol. 2 (Tokyo: Jinbutsu Ōraisha, 1965)

Nakanishi, Ritta, *A History of Japanese Armour* vol. 2 (Tokyo: Dainippon Kaiga, 2009)

Nishigaya, Yasuhiro, *Sengoku no jō 1:Kantō* (Tokyo: Gakken, 1993)

Odaka, Haruo, *Bōsō Satomi shi no jōkaku to kassen* (Tokyo: Ebisu Kōshō Shuppan, 2018)

Ōta, Tōshirō (ed.); Hanawa Hokinoichi (1746–1821), *Watanabe Suian oboegaki.* in *Zoku Gunsho Ruijū* vol. 20 (Tokyo: Zoku Gunsho Ruijū Kanseikai, 1923), pp.490–523

Owada, Tetsuo, *Imagawa Yoshimoto* (Tokyo: Minerva, 2004)

Parker, Geoffrey, *The Military Revolution: Military Innovation and the rise of the West 1500–1800* (Cambridge: Cambridge University Press, 1988)

Sadler, A.L., *The Maker of Modern Japan* (London: Allen and Unwin, 1937)

Sadler, A.L., *A Short History of Japan* (Sydney: Angus & Robertson, 1963)

Saitō, Shin'ichi, *Sengoku jidai no shūen: 'Hōjō no yume' to Hideyoshi no tenka tōitsu* (Tokyo: Yoshikawa Kōbukan, 2019)

Sansom, George, *A History of Japan 1334–1615* (London: The Cresset Press, 1961)

Sasaki, Michirō and Atsushi Chiba, *Sengoku Satake-shi kenkyū no saizensen* (Tokyo: Yamakawa Shuppansha, 2021)

Steenstrup, Carl, 'Hōjō Sōun's Twenty-One Articles: The Code of Conduct of the Odawara Hōjō', *Monumenta Nipponica* 29, 3, 1974, pp.283–303

Sugiyama, Hiroshi, *Nihon no Rekishi 11: Sengoku Daimyō* (Tokyo: Chūkō Bunko, 1974)

Sun, Laichen, 2003. 'Military Technology Transfers from Ming China and the Emergence of Northern Mainland Southeast Asia (*c.* 1390–1527)', *Journal of Southeast Asian Studies*, vol. 34, no. 3, 2003, pp.495–517

Sun, Laichen, 'Chinese Gunpowder Technology and Dai Viet, ca. 1390–1467', in Nhung Tuyet Tran and Anthony Reid (eds), *Viet Nam: Borderless Histories* (Madison: University of Wisconsin Press, 2006), pp.72–120

Suzuki, Masaya, *Teppō to Nihonjin* (Tokyo: Chikuma Shobō, 2000)

Swope, Kenneth, 'Crouching Tigers, Secret Weapons: Military Technology Employed during the Sino–Japanese–Korean War, 1592–1598', *The Journal of Military History*, 69, 1, 2005, pp.11–41

Takekoshi, Yosaburō, *The Economic Aspects of the History of the Civilisation of Japan* vol. 1 (London: Allen and Unwin, 1930)

Tamaru, Nobuaki (ed.), *Senryaku, Senjutsu, Heiki Jiten* (Tokyo: Gakken, 1994)

Thornton, S.A., '*Kōnodai senki*: Traditional Narrative and Warrior Ideology in Sixteenth-Century Japan', *Oral Tradition*, 15, 2, 2000, pp.306–376

Turnbull, Stephen, 'The ghosts of Amakusa: localised opposition to centralised control in Higo province, 1589–90', *Japan Forum* 25 2, 2012, pp.191–211

Turnbull, Stephen, *Tanaka 1587: Japan's Greatest Unknown Samurai Battle* (Warwick: Helion, 2019)

Turnbull, Stephen, 'Biting the Bullet: A Reassessment of the Development, Use and Impact of Early Firearms in Japan', *Vulcan, The Journal of the History of Military Technology* 8, 2020, pp.26–53

Turnbull, Stephen, *The Ōnin War: A Turning Point in Samurai History* (Warwick: Helion, 2021)

Turnbull, Stephen, *The Samurai Art of War as illustrated in Hōjō Godai ki* (independently published, 2021)

Udagawa, Takehisa, 'A photographic introduction to items from the collection', *Rekihaku* 126, 2006 <https://www.rekihaku.ac.jp/english/outline/publication/rekihaku/126/witness.html> (accessed 19 September 2022)

Udagawa, Takehisa (ed.), *Rekishi no naka no teppō denrai, Tanegashima kara Boshin sensō made*, second edition (Sakura City: Kokuritsu Rekishi Monzoku Hakubutsukan, 2007)

Udagawa, Takehisa, *Teppō denrai: heiki ga kataru kinsei no tanjō* (Tokyo: Kōdansha, 2013)

Umezawa, Takuo, *Matsuyama-jō kassen* (Matsuyama: Matsuyama Shobō, 2012)

Various authors, *Hōjō Godai ki: Rekishi Gunzō Series 14* (Tokyo: Gakken, 1989)

Walley, Glynne, *Eight Dogs, or Hakkenden. Part One – An Ill-Considered Jest* (New York: Cornell, 2021)

Yoshida, Yutaka (ed.), *Taikō ki* vols 1 and 3 (Tokyo: Kyōikusha, 1979)

Yuasa, Jōzan, *c.* 1853. *Jōzan Kidan* (1912 reprint) <https://archive.org/details/jozankidan00yuasuoft/page/n1> (accessed 22 July 2019)

Other titles in the From Retinue to Regiment series:

About the author

Stephen Turnbull took his first degree at Cambridge, and has two MAs (theology and military history) from Leeds University. In 1996 he received a PhD from Leeds for his thesis on Japan's 'Hidden Christians'. In its published form the work won the Japan Festival Literary Award in 1998. Having lectured widely in East Asian studies and theology he is now retired and pursues an active literary career, having published 90 books. His expertise has helped with numerous projects including films, television and the award-winning strategy game 'Shogun Total War'. He is currently working on a major new study for Helion about warfare in early modern Southeast Asia, focussing on the impact of firearms and the use of war elephants.

About the artists

Emmanuel Valerio was born in 1960 in the Philippines and studied architecture in college. He moved to Canada in 1979 and lives in Surrey, British Columbia, painting portraits and wildlife art. He has worked on covers for wargaming, science fiction and military history books. He is also a miniatures sculptor of samurai and the American Plains Indians for both commercial companies and private collectors. He has spent 35 years researching and illustrating samurai heraldry, sharing his work online in 'The Samurai Archives Forum'. In 2018, he wrote and illustrated a chapter for David F. Phillips' book *Japanese Heraldry and Heraldic Flags*.

Anderson Subtil was born in Curitiba, southern Brazil, and holds a degree in drawing from the School of Music and Fine Arts of the Paraná State. Since 2018, he has worked as an illustrator for several of the Helion & Company series. His artworks have been published in books and magazines in Brazil, the United States, the United Kingdom, France, Austria and Japan.